Belief
Beyond Belief

Looking to a Better Future

Alistair J. Sinclair Ph.D.

AP
Almostic

Almostic Publications
2017

Published by
Almostic Publications
Glasgow
ISBN 978-0-9574044-8-9

Other Works by
Alistair J. Sinclair

BOOKS

The Answers Lie Within Us
What is Philosophy: An Introduction
The Will to Live: A Systematic Guide to Our Reasons for Living
American Papers in Humanism and Religion
Sautonic Wisdom: What We Are Here To Do
The Promise of Dualism: An Introduction to Dualist Theory
Hale and Hearty: Looking at Things as a Whole
Advancing Humanity: The Need to Make Our Own Future

E-BOOKS

The Future of Humanity: The Need to Believe in Humanity and its Future
Vindication: Justifying Our Existence
From Time to Eternity: An Essay on the Meaning of Time
Shakespeare on Time
Punish the Person not the Crime: A New Theory of Punishment Based on
Old Principles
Old Age, Death and the After-Life
Reforming the British Constitution
The Normal Society: And How To Get It

Dedicated

To all the religions that have contributed to humanity's spiritual advancement, but which have now had their day.
(Symbolised on the front cover)

Dedicated

To all the nations that have unified their peoples and brought them forward but which must now give way to the increasing unity of humanity. (Symbolised on the back cover)

Dedicated

To the increasing mixture of the races that will soon disappear into the melting pot of humanity

Contents

Part One – The Meaning of Belief

Part Two – The Purpose of Belief

Foreword

This book offers a humanistic alternative to religion that does not demand absolute belief. It may interest those who are not religious minded but who want to believe in something. It is not intended to undermine anyone's religious faith but only to show that losing one's faith is not the end of the story. Having no belief in God does not necessarily mean believing in nothing. Having no religious faith does not mean having a complete lack of faith. This view can broaden one's outlook, as more is being ruled in than is being ruled out by the holistic view that is here advocated. It forms a comprehensive belief system called 'prospectivism' which is introduced in this book. The prospective view is both inclusive and all-embracing. It looks to the future with the past in mind.

Religion does not have a monopoly on belief or faith; even without it there is still much to believe in. This book suggests that, apart from our political and scientific beliefs, we can also believe in life, humanity and their future. We can reinforce our beliefs by valuing life and humanity and by being true to them. We can believe that there is a future for them despite all the real or imagined threats to their future. These are qualified rather than absolute beliefs as they depend on the evidence and on our constant scepticism concerning whether we are justified in holding such beliefs.

This is a prospective view oriented towards the future instead of clinging entirely to the past like the traditional religions and nationalist ideologies. It takes a holistic view of all the diverse views and is therefore inclusive unlike the exclusive view typical of most religions and ideologies. It is moreover a philosophy to be explored rather than a viewpoint to be adhered to in any absolute sense. It is intended to be suggestive and thought-provoking. We do not worship life and humanity but rather study and contemplate them in the widest terms worthy of philosophy. The hope is that by such a measured regard for life and humanity, we can come together as a unified and co-operative species in pursuit of our common ends and thus work towards a better future for us all.

Introduction

The Prospective View

Belief in life and humanity offers the best possible foundation for a dynamic, holistic belief system that looks to the future. It is a 'belief beyond belief' in that it goes beyond belief, especially religious belief. This is not to eliminate religious beliefs, but rather to make use of them as they are mines of information about human nature and its history. Religions are to be understood sympathetically rather than believed in absolutely. This is the rationale of the comparative religion movement of the 20th century. That movement compared and contrasted all religions without focusing on any particular religion as being better or more desirable than any of the rest. Thus, prospectivism is a post-religious belief system that takes the widest possible perspective and is inclusive of all religions without being a religion itself. We enrich and enlighten ourselves better by studying religions from afar than by imprisoning ourselves in one 'faith' to the exclusion of all others.

Cynics, sceptics, nihilists and pessimists may pour scorn on our belief in life and humanity but they often believe in nothing at all. Even if the future of life and humanity is forever in doubt, we can still believe in them and act accordingly. With sufficient self-confidence in our role in the universe we don't need the support of external beings such as gods, aliens whose existence depends entirely on the imagination of their beholders. This book aims to bolster and justify that self-confidence so that such imaginary crutches are no longer needed.

Thus, this prospective view looks forward to a better future rather than dwelling on the failings of the past. It looks forward also to the increasing unity and orderliness which both life and humanity bring into the universe. This unity and orderliness trends towards a *cosmic unity* that has emerged from the natural processes of the universe. It is greatly accelerated by the growing purposefulness of living beings. This is not God but a purposeful trend in the material universe leading to the potential unity of the universe. Entities come together naturally by the four forces of physics, namely, the strong and weak atomic forces, and the electro-magnetic and gravitational forces. Each entity comprises a unified pocket of orderliness and harmony during its existence. Life and humanity themselves result from these unifying processes of the universe, as is described in astronomy, biology and the other sciences (for more on this see pages 54-60 below). The ubiquity of this unifying activity throughout the universe is thus confirmed by scientific research. In these respects, prospectivism is wholly compatible with what science tells us about the universe. We are all products of universal processes that are trending towards this cosmic unity and we all can make our individual contributions to that trend.

Contributing to greater cosmic unity gives us goals by which we can make our mark on the universe. All our rational and social activities have this overall purpose of bringing more order and unity into being. Even our most trivial acts are more significant in this universal light. For example, the simple act of tidying one's home creates order that didn't exist before. More importantly, technological advances make the building of railways, bridges, houses, and office blocks more orderly and organised. We save time, materials, human effort and become more purposeful and unified in our activities. All this activity contributes incrementally to the greater purpose by which we bring more unity and order into the universe. (The diagram on page 55 gives a rough view of the trend towards cosmic unity in which we are participating with our orderly and rational activities.)

Moreover, our very sociability contributes to cosmic unity. The more we do for each other, the better we can live together and work together to achieve great and worthwhile things. Thus, the role of service is important in the prospective view of things. We serve each other and society at large. In so doing we add meaning and purpose to our lives and those of others. The role of service is the subject of section 4 (see pages 39-53).

The relationship between life and humanity is also extremely important. We are intimately and interactively connected with life and *vice versa*. The future of life on this planet depends greatly on humanity responsibly fulfilling its role as caretaker of the planet. Life is more important than humanity in so far as life will survive humanity's extinction. It is far more ubiquitous on this planet than humanity. Even if we are wiped out, life in some form is almost certain to survive *e.g.* bacteria, fungi, sea-life of all kinds, insects, and rats. Life in general is so important to us that we may even give our lives for its survival in all its forms; just as we give our lives for other people, or for causes greater than ourselves. Thus, the continuing interrelationship between life and humanity is vital to this belief system.

Getting Beyond Religion

If humanity is to make real and lasting progress, we must get beyond religion. This does not mean undermining people's faith; it means going beyond the exclusivity of religion that looks down on other beliefs instead of trying to understand them. We need a post-religious view that embraces all religions and eliminates the rivalry and hatred engendered by their differences. Adhering to one religion to the exclusion of all others bolsters beliefs such as the following: that prophets were inspired by angels to write sacred texts, as believed by Mormons and Mohammedans; that extraterrestrials created or influenced the human race, as believed by Raelians and Scientologists; that people rise from the dead and be the 'Son of God', as believed by Christians; that people can reach a higher state of consciousness by spiritual exercises of one sort or another, as believed by Buddhists and New Ageists. Those who believe in such things in an exclusive way are treating such beliefs as inviolable truths. They disparage the disbelievers and have contempt for other faiths. We cannot move forward together while the various religions remain at loggerheads with each other and we lack common ends and goals by which we can work together for a better future.

Post-religion means not adhering to one religious system and excluding all the rest. It means embracing all that humanity has to offer in the way of spirituality and self-belief. Religion can narrow our emotions, whereas post-religion can liberate them. Prospectivism is post-religious in being dynamic and holistic; it constantly looks at things as a whole and is always looking to rethink and update beliefs in a manner worthy of science. Thus, prospectivism is an attitude of mind more than a fixed creed. It looks at what the scientific view means for our future. That view tells us that there is no place for God in the universe. We have reached the stage where we have outgrown the need for such an imaginary entity. Though there is no purpose in the physical workings of the universe, nevertheless life and humanity bring purpose into existence. Such beliefs behind prospective thinking are constantly up for review.

The prospective-minded person is open to the future and uses the past to make the future better. In contrast, the typical religious-minded person is rooted in the past and wishes it to continue changelessly into the future. Everyone can become prospective-minded (1) by opening their minds to all religious points of view instead of being cripplingly confined to one belief to the exclusion of all others, and (2) by putting the plight of humanity before purely religious concerns that undermine humanity instead of inspiring it to better things in the future.

The Role of Prospectivist Beliefs

Beliefs are here treated as the *subject* of our study rather than the *object*. Religion typically objectifies its objects. Sacred texts are objectified as being god-given when they are really the products of human ingenuity – thus insulting our integrity as inventive beings. Repetitive rituals and ceremonies are obsessively adhered to as if they had an objective life of their own. Words are treated as if they have an objective reality; prayers are a kind of abject begging to nonexistent entities and they supposedly change the real world. Such extreme objectivity is the ruin of personal belief. If we allow our beliefs to become totally objective, they become absolute and indisputable. They are made out to be true for everyone, everywhere, and they become exclusive to whatever group or organisation that adheres to them. In contrast, when we treat beliefs subjectively, they remain personal to us, and relative to what we feel about them. A constant interaction between the subjective and objective can keep us in touch with reality. For real and lasting knowledge enables us to interact successfully with the real world, as indeed scientific knowledge enables us to do.

Prospective beliefs, in particular, involve an interactive quest for truth whereas exclusive religious beliefs are treated as the objective truth. We want to appreciate all religious beliefs without focusing on one to the exclusion of all others. All such beliefs are of interest in our holistically understanding humanity. Prospectivism encourages this because of its inclusive nature. If we believe in life and humanity, we also appreciate all the influences that have made what the human race is today, even though we need not believe in them.

In any case, objectivity proper belongs to impersonal knowledge that is certain and reliable when it is shown to be applicable. Science is objective when it is based on reliable knowledge, usually expressed mathematically or symbolically. Belief in God can only be personal and never amount to impersonal knowledge, unless evidence for its existence can be found that is universally acknowledged, but such evidence cannot be found as the notion is cultural and not based on scientific fact or on the way that the universe is constructed.

The Practice of Belief

Believing in life, humanity and the future can give meaning to our lives provided we work hard in developing these beliefs. The more reasons we have to practise these beliefs the more meaningful they are to us. The first part of this book therefore elaborates what is meant by believing in these things. It is important to believe in life and humanity because they both have so much to offer the universe. Life is the salvation of the universe. It saves the universe from being nothing but a boring assemblage of material objects that make no sense in themselves. It does not need the support of entities such as gods and aliens that exist only in our imagination. It uses its own inner resources to survive and thrive. The burgeoning and complexifying of life makes possible the universe's unified recreation and its continuation in another form in the far future. Life may achieve amazing things by continuing its complexification beyond our present achievements. Humanity is thus important as it is at present the universe's only means of seeing itself and justifying its own existence.

Believing in life and humanity involves commitment, justification, understanding, self-knowledge, and service, but it is entirely up to the individual to decide the extent to which they want to involve themselves in that belief. We can all serve life and humanity in the ways that suit our individuality and uniqueness as human beings. Thus, service is an important component of the prospective view and it is dealt with in more detail in section four of this book.

This belief system does not require the existence of any supernatural being that is supposed to be responsible for our being here. It disputes the value of believing in the existence of immaterial beings that diminish our responsibility for ourselves and our lives. God is the source for much evil in the world as people are still harming and even killing each other in its name. Belief in its existence causes enmity and divisions in god-believing religions as a generally accepted notion of what it is or is not has proved elusive. Also, belief in an unknown and unknowable God impedes the search for our inner being, namely, what makes us unique and irreplaceable human beings. In short, the very idea of God, whatever it is, does us more harm than good.

We can study religion without believing in it or in the existence of God. We can appreciate the contribution of religion to human life in the past. This is not to rubbish religion but to show its true place in our culture. That place does not consist in telling people how to live their lives but in helping them to work out for themselves the best way to live. All religions have something to say about this, and none is the sole answer. The study of religion is laudable but its practice can do more harm than good. The value of religion and god belief becomes questionable when they are used to exert social control over people and to prevent them from thinking out things for themselves.

The Purpose of this Book

In my book *The Will to Live: A Systematic Guide to our Reasons for Living*, I explore a range of questions such as: 'What are we here for?', 'What can we do with our lives?' and 'Why should we live at all?' It gives a wide assortment of answers to these questions. In this book, I am concerned about our reasons for believing, and in particular why we should believe in life, humanity and the future. Questions are addressed such as: 'What is important about life?' 'What is important about humanity?', 'Why has life come into being?' and 'What is the role of humanity in the universe?' Assumptions are made such as the following:

❖ Belief in life and humanity implies that there is a future for these and that they will not necessarily die out any time soon.
❖ There is no purpose in the universe except the purposes introduced into it by life forms pursuing the ends of their own fashioning.
❖ The ultimate purpose of life is to bring increasing order into an increasing chaotic universe.
❖ The ultimate purpose of humanity is to create an orderly cosmos containing its achievements.

We don't normally believe in anything to no purpose. We usually make use of our beliefs, as belief is meant to be a prelude to action, otherwise it is insincere. In applying our beliefs to some worthy end or other, we make more of them. In the case of prospectivism, the end is a better future for all humanity and all life-forms. A better future for ourselves ensures a better future for life as whole. We harm ourselves when we threaten the future of life on this planet, as we are doing by damaging the environment.

We need also to understand better what it means to be human. It is possible that we may 'improve' people by genetic modification, by enhancing our brain powers, or by 'transhuman' or computer-generated means. But whenever we leave our humanity behind by such means we are in uncharted waters. It is comparable to our 'god-like' aspirations by which we are likely to become diabolical and inhuman in our behaviour. Science fiction writers constantly warn us about how inhuman we can become by being more than human, one way or another. It would be better and saner to improve our views of what it is to be human, as is attempted in this book.

In conclusion, therefore, prospectivism is about seeing that we are a part of the whole. It is a holistic view in which we can take comfort from contemplating the extent of our interconnections with the universe and everything that is in it. It is also about working out for ourselves what we are here for. The meaning and purpose of our lives may be found by a trial-and-error process that involves making ourselves useful to others, exploring the world, thinking about how life and humanity have evolved from the matter and energy of the universe, understanding the nature of civilisation, and generally doing things to improve ourselves, both mentally and physically. This is a philosophical interpretation of what science is telling us about the universe and our relationship to it. It is therefore more than just a scientific view since it goes beyond science to offer a coherent philosophy of what we are and what we are here to do.

The prospective belief system is also about getting things done. This includes the following aims:

❖ To make the human race a self-regarding family instead of an antagonistic assembly of races, religions, nations, organisations, groups, tribes, sects, gangs or cabals.

❖ To create the conditions in which everyone can work together for the common ends of life and humanity instead of pursuing narrow ends that cause conflict and enmity between lesser groupings of people.

❖ To further and foster life both on this planet and elsewhere. We need to come together if we are to make a better future for all humankind, preserve life on Earth, and ultimately spread it throughout the universe.

❖ To bring joy and laughter into life and human affairs. Believing in life and humanity means also looking at the bright side of things and finding consolation in even the most adverse of circumstances. On the other hand, to expect nothing else from life but joy and laughter is to invite the opposite reaction – despair and despondency. Moderation in all things may be boring but like honesty it is the best policy.

❖ To console ourselves and others in the face of death that whatever we experience and achieve in life is carried forward and never dies. Though there is no afterlife, our lives are nevertheless are impregnated on the fabric of the universe.

Our belief in life, humanity and their future can also be rationalised under the following headings that outline prospectivism as a whole:

An Outline of the Prospective System

I. The Meaning of Belief

1. Life
a. creates its own meaning
b. justifies itself in the universe
c. belief in it counters materialism

2.Humanity
a. a post religious belief that is not worshipful
b. self-belief makes us important
c. the Optimist's Creed

3. Future
a. prospectivism is future-oriented
b. the view of posterity orients us to the future
c. posterity is omnipresent

II. The Purpose of Belief

4. Service
a. serving life and humanity
b. service by counselling
c. the roles of service

5. Cosmic Unity
a. the unifying process of the universe
b. the importance of the holistic view
c. the unifying cosmos

Improving Prospective Exercises
(see pages 48-50):

1. *Vitality:* The knowledge and development of our inner vitality is necessary to achieve self-fulfilment.
2. *Illuminosity:* Light is all important to life and humanity since the light of the sun makes life possible on Earth. We illuminate things by clarification and enlightenment.
3. *Creativity:* What makes humanity important on this planet is our creativity. We bring into being new things that never existed before.
4. *Morality:* To serve life and be served by it, we need to be self-disciplined which entails self-discipline and having a moral viewpoint to live by.

Enhancing Prospective Exercises
(see pages 50-53):

1. *Emergence – How life came to the fore:* Life and humanity are products of the ever growing complexity of the universe.
2. *Duality – Seeking the Middle Way:* Life and humanity are products of the dualist interactions that characterise the universe. We live in a dualistic world in which we must cope with constant contrasts between extremes such as good and evil.
3. *Centrality – Living at the centre of things:* We are important because we occupy the middle position between the very small and the very large.

Part One
The Meaning of Belief

1. Believing in Life

The First Principle of Prospectivism

Having a belief in life encourages us to bring our own meaning into existence without which the universe is meaningless in every respect. By such meaning we ensure that our future differs from our past.

Life is the crowning glory of the Earth. Some may disagree. They see life as a festering slime on the surface of the Earth. But this is a narrow view. When we put life into the context of the universe as a whole, we can see its importance. It is the ultimate culmination of inner complexity that gives our planet the majesty and enthronement that few planets possess. Life arose through an ever-increasing internal complexity brought about by purposeful activity. It doesn't need justification outside itself – it did it all by itself without divine intervention. (See pages 54-60 for more on this.)

The idea of life is unique to intelligent beings. We are like other life-forms in struggling for life and in enjoying it when we can. However, we are not like other life-forms on this planet in that we can think of life as an abstract notion whereas they live their lives without knowing what life is. We know not only what life is but also how important it is. Only intelligent beings like ourselves know that life is at the apogee of entity existence in the universe. Life-forms are more complexified than other entities. As a result, life has more to offer the universe in terms of purposefulness than other less complexified entities. For that reason, life is worth fighting for to ensure that it is sustained and that its propagation throughout the universe is maintained. Thus, our primary self-appointed purpose must be to support that propagation of life. Admittedly, that process has scarcely begun as our ability to exploit outer space is still in its infancy.

Believing in life implies that life has some meaning. Life in the abstract has meaning because it refers to the most complex forms of entity in the universe. We can admire and revere life because of its unique position in the universe. But our own lives as individuals are even more important to us. These lives stand in most need of belief and meaningfulness. For life *means* what we think it is, and the act of giving our lives meaning is precisely what we are living to do. The fact is that we make our own meaning in life, so that the meaning of life is the meaning we put into it, get out of it, make of it or find in it. What we do with our lives confers meaning on them. Our lives have no meaning at all in isolation from what we make of them. We might choose to regard everything we do as meaningless and fruitless but that is only a choice and is not the whole truth of the matter. We may choose to think of our lives as being meaningless when we are in the mood to do so. But that does not make

9

them so. Seeing everything as meaningless is a matter of emotional mood: it is an attitude that changes as readily as all our moods do. A suicidal frame of mind similarly depends on our being in the mood for it and when the mood passes the need to do it fades away, even if only temporarily. Many people who survive their suicide attempts go on to live satisfying lives. To avoid such states of mind, we must continually make the effort to find and create meaning. The truth always includes the other side of the coin, or indeed the silver lining to the dark cloud.

As life forms, we are the creators of meaning in the universe. It can never be repeated too often that there is no meaning in the universe except that which is brought into existence by living beings pursuing their ingiven purposes. They require no external agents to provide meaning or to give them the power to find meaning. They arrive at meanings *firstly* to preserve and prolong their existence as identifiable and distinguishable entities and *secondly* to nourish and enrich their lives. Their inner complexity is such that it requires such meaningfulness to preserve their being and make sense of their lives. Otherwise their unity and integrity would only be short lived and they would be unable to pass on their inner complexity through reproduction or cultural dissemination. It is the complexity of the inner interactions that makes living beings distinct from mere material objects that lack a life of their own. (See pages 52-53 for more on the role of complexity in bringing life into being.)

Meaning means doing. In common with all living beings, human beings find meaning by doing things and this makes us doers or agents. Doing involves interacting. We connect with things and make them meaningful to ourselves by that connection. If I touch a table with a fingertip, I interact with it by means of nerve impulses that are activated by contact with table's surface, and these impulses travel back and forth between the fingertip and my brain. The impulses convey and confirm the feeling which the act of touching gives me. The feeling has meaning for me because I have interacted with something distinct from myself. I identify with the object because of that feeling which is mine alone. Interacting thus involves meaning when the agent finds it in the act of feeling, seeing, speaking, writing, or whatever. Thus, the ultimate meaning of life for each of us lies in doing things which are meaningful to us. In everything that we do for a reason, we are creating meaning that did not previously exist.

In creating meaning we become responsible for the future of all life, since everything that we do has ramifications that stretch near and far, and perhaps in ways beyond our present comprehension, as quantum physics seems to tell us. The meaning created by intelligent beings is also important in that it is self-reflective and self-critical. By self-examination, we can ascertain the value of what we are doing and the good and bad effects of our deeds. This implies that intelligent beings such as ourselves are the most accountable of all entities in the universe. Our self-awareness makes us responsible for our surroundings. Seeing the plight of our planet makes us want to do something about it. We become responsible for life because we know what life means for the future of the universe. Without the burgeoning of life in the universe, it has no meaning. As the future of life is always precarious, we can give meaning to our lives by dedicating ourselves to the cultivation and propagation of life. We then become responsible for the plight of life in the universe and can justify our existence by doing everything we can to nurture life and further it. That responsibility cannot be shirked without denying our self-knowledge of what we are and underestimating what we can do as a species, as many pro-religionists and anti-humanists are prone to do in undermining our status in this universe.

How life finds meaning in the universe. The vastness of the universe is an opportunity for life and humanity and not a drawback. Science teaches us that we live in a huge and entirely material universe that is subject to unique physical laws and arbitrary chance events. From that point of view, the universe means nothing at all apart from the chance and necessity of events that govern it. We and other living beings are only tiny, tenuous vestiges of self-awareness in an otherwise vast and indifferent material universe. But these are not dismal facts when we consider that the vast amounts of matter and energy are an endless resource for living beings to tap into. In a manner of speaking, we are seeded into this vast universe and have only begun to grow. This fact encourages us to use this resource to our own ends since there is apparently nothing in the universe to prevent us from doing except our own inertia and lack of self-belief. We can therefore accept our material insignificance with cheerful equanimity when we consider that how meaningful and joyful we can make our lives regardless of such material considerations.

The Self-Justifying Theory of the Universe.

Life is important to the universe because it enables the universe to achieve self-justification. The simplest and most appealing explanation for the existence of the universe and the emergence of living beings is that the universe is self-referential and self-contained. Nothing else is required to explain its existence. It came into being so that there was something rather than nothing. There is something so that there can be something called 'existence'. Without life, the universe has no means of justifying itself; it exists only in itself. We are so much a part of it that we cannot deny its existence without denying our own existence in the process. Life enables the universe to refer back to itself and assert its existence. In short, life is the vehicle by which the universe achieves self-justification. All this follows from the fact that we are inextricably part of the universe and are therefore involved in it.

The physical laws of the universe have made this self-justification possible by forging its contents into discrete unities so that they may be identified and distinguished as entities in their own right. These physical laws are necessary to make possible the increasing complexification of its contents. We are the ultimate products of this self-justifying process and therefore have the opportunity to justify ourselves accordingly by making sense of the universe and carving our own place in it. There is an obvious circularity involved whereby our being able to justify its existence gives the universe the potential to exist and continue existing. Thus, our justifying our own existence leads to our justifying the existence of the universe.

The universe came into existence because it could exist and thus had the potential to exist. Similarly, everything that came into existence in the beginning had the potential to exist. Potentiality precedes actuality. Everything that happens in the universe occurs because it has the potential to happen. That potential is not pre-ordained nor does it always require chance or necessity. In the case of life and humanity, there is the possibility of choices, decisions, goals, so that activity can go in different directions depending on the inner choices made by living beings.

As the universe is self-contained in its existing, it needs no external agency to bring it into being or to maintain its existence. As we exist ourselves, it is incumbent on us to find our own justification for existing. We do so by the meaning, value, interest and purposefulness that we introduce by the mere fact of living. We are meant to be here because of the meaning we demonstrably put into our lives, the lives of others and the universe at large. This is our cosmic purpose as compared with our mundane material existence on this planet. Therefore, the meaning of our lives is also self-referential because we are responsible for giving our lives the meaning they otherwise lack.

Does the universe have meaning and value whether we exist or do not exist? It certainly exists physically whether we exist or not. We know this because of the evidence of its past existence and the fact that other people die just as we are going to die and the world goes on as it was, despite that sad fact. But the universe can also be meaningful, despite our disappearance as a species, because of its potential to be meaningful to some intelligent species or other. To mean anything the universe must be represented in words, symbols and images such as living beings alone are capable of creating. As it can be described in communicable words and symbols, it has the potential for meaning and value for whatever living beings exist in it. The universe is then meaningful as a place to live in whenever it has living beings in it and the potential for intelligent beings living on distant planets. We humans can also value its meaningfulness in our imagining ourselves not existing in it. In picturing a universe without our existing in it, we are already conferring meaning and value on it. But it is always we who are creating that meaning and value in our representations of it. The meaning and value do not really exist outside our imaginations or those of other intelligent beings.

We believe that the universe continues to exist without us when we die or become extinct, as we have our reasons to believe that it will continue to exist whether we are here or not. Only our lack of complete knowledge of what might happen in the future makes such an assumption doubtful. We cannot know with absolute certainty that it can exist without human beings to create order and make some sense of it. There is a subtle interaction going on here which is beyond our total understanding. The suspicion is that some of the ordering of the universe is due to our being here to create that order. This has some basis in reality because of the fact that we do bring meaning and value into being, even though it is only in our thinking about it. In acting on our beliefs, we change reality and so the more meaningful we make the universe, the more we have the potential to change it and bring more reason and order into it.

Thus, it is arguable that the universe itself can be made more orderly by our rational activities. It has the order that we conceive it to have because we are capable of ordering it in that way through our scientific understanding of it. Whether there is any more to the universe than what science and common sense tell us is all speculation without the possibility of proof, one way or the other. For instance, the idea that parallel universes exist when there is no sign of them for us to see, touch, hear, or feel is pure speculation based on mathematical theories unsupported by direct evidence. As things stand, their existence is no more credible than the existence of God, and people's belief in them is akin to religious belief.

We don't know what the ultimate answers are, but we can get nearer to them in time, but only if we continue doggedly to seek them. Though our descendants may acquire an ever greater understanding of what life is all about, the full explanation may elude even them. That is a challenge and not a disaster. Life is not so much a mystery to be explained as a miracle to be lived. The fact of our living at all is miraculous enough without our having to know what it is all about. But it is a miracle that is due to an exceedingly unlikely concatenation of events. We need no longer feel indebted to a creator of any kind. We can now live our lives from the inside out instead of feeling at the mercy of supernatural forces and influences that have no basis in fact. By coming to terms with our inner needs it is possible to convince ourselves that we have not lived in vain. Hopefully this book helps to make this process of inner self-reliance a living reality for everyone.

Belief in Life Counters Materialism.

Contemplating life and realising its importance to the universe gives us a holist view that transcends the materialistic view in our society. That view narrows people's thinking so that they are obsessed not only with possessing material goods but also with a mindless commitment to the rat race. Too many people sell their souls to their jobs, careers, pop idols, or hobbies to the exclusion of the wider perspective. In narrowing their interests and pre-occupations to progressively fewer things, they lose touch with the wider unifying theme to which everything belongs. This unifying theme is not God or anything supernatural but whatever results from our sharing what we all have in common as human beings, that is to say, the life that lies within each of us. This 'inner being' brings us together as integrated personalities and helps us to cultivate the good that is within us. This involves universalising our moral concepts whereby we realise and appreciate our connections with other people. We reach inside ourselves in order to reach out to other people. This 'inner being' is supervenient rather than supernatural. It emerges from our materiality on which it supervenes and develops organically. The meaning and consequences of this 'inner being' are dealt with in more depth in my other works, particularly in *Advancing Humanity* (2016) and *Hale and Hearty* (2016).

In narrowing people's interests and pre-occupations, a materialistic attitude leads to short-termism. It shortens time scales and prevents people from delaying their choices. Instant gratification and an endless succession of transitory pleasures becomes the norm. What seems important and valuable at the present moment is immediately sought, bought, experienced, or fulfilled. The lessons of past experience are forgotten, and new experiences add nothing to one's life as a whole.

In a materialist frame of mind, people are unable to put their needs and desires into a context which puts them at arm's length. Everything is related to themselves and their immediate needs, desires and impulses. They may even think of themselves as mere animals and behave accordingly. Their needs and desires predominate, and they become enslaved by them. They make more and more out of less and less, and then forfeit their freedom to be themselves. In crowding their lives with trivia, they lose sight of what is of real and lasting importance in life. The latter is as much spiritual as material, since it includes the value and importance of human relationships, as well as the bigger things in life, such as the universe as a whole.

Our lives, and the quality we bring into them, are of greater importance than the material surroundings in which we live them. Unless we have a realistic view of the value of material objects, relative to our own value as human beings, there seems little point in having them. Such knowledge is a personal matter that has no lasting material existence outside our thinking about it.

A bias towards materialism can be blamed on the failure of religious teaching to maintain the balance between the inner and outer viewpoints, as religion is traditionally biased towards spiritual matters. It is argued here that the strength and comfort of our inner well-being need no longer be sought in dogmatic beliefs but in the process of looking into ourselves and evaluating our inner life. We begin exploring our inner being when we attempt to make sense of the values that we attach to our subjective feelings and experiences. This is a first step towards satisfying ourselves about the ultimate value of our lives. This view is developed further in part two of this book.

However, in stressing the importance of inner being, the value of the material world is not thereby rejected. Material comfort and secure living are required to ensure that our inner values can flourish and develop. A bed of nails or fanatical asceticism does little or nothing for our intuitive creativity. Yet many religions still advocate penances, fasts, flagellation, and other forms of self-punishment as the way to faith and to set oneself right with God. Thus, we must guard against going from one extreme of material comfort to another extreme of physical mortification. The view being developed here eschews such extremes because our inner being is here seen as an activity directed towards ends. It is not treated an end in itself to the extremes of mindless meditation and endless contemplation.

Belief in life is not an absolute belief. We can believe in the potential of life without believing that it must be preserved for its own sake. Death is such a part of life that the preservation and prolongation of life in all circumstances whatsoever is unrealistic and unnecessary. Medical doctors often make life or death decisions in such matters as abortion and near death situations. It is difficult if not impossible to prevent people from committing suicide if they are really intent upon it. However, the general principle is that life is worth preserving and prolonging for its own sake. The exceptions to that rule can never be stated, laid down or enforced without putting us on the slippery slope towards favouring death, execution or suicide for their own sakes. The various 'Doctor Deaths' killing their patients, the various revolutions involving the likes of Robespierre, Pol Pot, and Stalin that eliminate undesirables, the Holocaust that eliminated Jews, are all examples of killing allegedly justified on rational grounds. We have to believe that life is so valuable that we hesitate to bring it to an end for whatever reason. But there are no hard and fast rules to guide us as each case has to be considered in its context and from all points of view.

2. Believing in Humanity

The Second Principle of Prospectivism

A belief in humanity means believing in humanity's future despite all the problems and difficulties facing us, and despite our limited powers and any incompetence and stupidity we display in dealing with our problems.

A belief in humanity is necessary for our future. If we don't believe in its future, then there is no point in our planning for the future. This belief is usually implicit in our purposeful activities. Each time something new is planned and carried out – whether in politics, business, architecture, medicine or whatever – a belief that humanity will survive into the foreseeable future is implied. Everyday life depends on such a belief.

If we agree that humanity is the highest form of intelligent life that we know of as yet, then we can hardly avoid believing in its future, even if we are doubtful of that future. There is always something going wrong with the world and when we concentrate too much on the insanities we see around us, it is difficult to believe in humanity's future. We must take the broadest possible view and consider that humanity has always been on a knife edge between accomplishing great things and destroying itself completely.

Moreover, we need a steadfast belief in humanity and its future to ensure that we do indeed have a future. Practically everything we do has some future consequences that imply at least some belief in our future. The optimistic view goes further and assumes that humanity has a good chance of surviving into the far future. The chances of our being obliterated by comets, solar flares or other cosmic catastrophes are fairly slim. Also, we don't expect humanity to stupidly destroy itself through its own malevolent self-destructiveness. We must work hard to stave off such self-destructiveness, the potential for which lurks in every corner of our civilisation.

There is also the optimistic belief in the inevitable propagation of life throughout the universe and in our potential role in contributing to that propagation. Belief in humanity and its future is a prerequisite to that propagation since, in the absence of other means, we alone have the technical ability to do it. Such beliefs are fundamental but they are not absolute as they are contingent upon our actually doing things to ensure our future. They are also contingent on humanity being worthy of any future at all. Its deserving to have any future has always been in doubt. We need continuously to work hard to justify our existence on this planet.

These are not just matters of opinion. They are empirical matters which may be shown to be the case by careful and impartial consideration

16

of the facts. It is a fact that humanity has developed the ability to look into the future and question whether it can survive into the far future. When we look at the state of humanity at any point in time its future has always been in doubt. Plagues and other natural catastrophes have decimated our species, yet it has survived even though the odds may have been stacked against it. Whether we will continue to survive and thrive is always a matter of probability. But we can always find reasons for optimism if we want to find them. Whether we deign to face the fact that we will probably survive into the future is also a matter of choice.

There is no point in being wise unless it is for some purpose beyond ourselves. In the absence of any credible supernatural being, that purpose can consist in making a worthwhile contribution to humanity and its future. If we do anything meaningful in our lives, it is in the implicit expectation that it will have meaning in the future and that humanity will survive in the future. There is no need for anyone to explicitly believe in humanity's future. That belief is implicit in everything we do whether we are conscious of it or not. If what we do makes sense to others then we are taking part in human affairs by doing rational and sensible things. The fact that we are human beings, taking part in the activities of the human race, is also an implicit acknowledgement of this belief. No one needs to be put to the test about this as it is plain in the actions of even the most sceptical or misanthropic of persons. If they behave rationally and do human things in their everyday lives, they show themselves to be as human as the rest of us.

Thus, belief in humanity is unavoidable whether it is implicit or explicit. The whole of humanity depends on everyone contributing in their own small way to that whole. We cannot make such contributions unless we think at least occasionally in global terms, as we do, for example, in the various anti-poverty campaigns and in our concerns for the victims of earthquakes, tsunamis, floods and famines. These arguments therefore show the importance of our getting together to ensure our own future which depends on all of us not only worrying about it from time to time but also doing something about it.

The dualist nature of humanity. The notion of humanity is not just inclusive of every human being. It also consists in what the individual human being contributes to it and what it can do for the individual in return. The interaction between these is what makes the human race work. We are dualist beings who are constantly interacting with ourselves and with others. We can use the notion of humanity to enhance our interactions with people. Thus, humanity is only an idea or notion and is not more important than the individual person. Our contribution to humanity is what we do in making the most of what we are as individual human beings. What humanity can do for us is to give us the opportunity to do our best as human beings. This includes our rights and responsibilities as mentioned in section four on *Serving Life and Humanity.* Thus, humanity is not an end in itself but a means of benefiting us all as individuals. It ceases to benefit us when it lets anyone down unnecessarily.

But why should we worry about the future of humanity, let alone believe in it? Most people never think about it from one day to the next. We are too concerned about our own present worries. The idea that humanity as a whole has a future, as opposed to the future of our respective races, nations, religions, organisations or other divisions, does not loom large among our concerns. Yet our everyday lives depend on the human race moving forward to better things. As argued above, if we don't progress we will regress to a worse kind of society. The forward movement unites us as a species and we make progress because the sense of direction gives us a common purpose. Without that, we will fall apart and start fighting each other as has happened so often in the past, and is still happening in many parts of the world even today. Working together to secure humanity's future gives us a common purpose, as does spreading life beyond Earth.

The worry is that, as a species, we can regress very easily to a more primitive state. If the idea of humanity fails to unify us, our society will sooner or later disintegrate into antagonistic units – nations competing to destroy other nations – religions fighting against other religions – races exterminating other races. There is no limit to the regression of humanity to more primitive conditions if we lose contact with each other and become insular groups that gradually forget their past traditions and ways of doing things. The Tasmanian aborigines and the Tierra Fuegans (mentioned by Darwin in his book *The Voyage of 'The Beagle'*) are examples of how isolated groups can lose their skills and forget how to fish and make fire. Archaeological evidence clearly shows that their ancestors had these skills in their dim and distant past.

Anthropological research shows the mechanisms of increasing distrust and over-self-sufficiency leads to the breakdown of social structures and a regression of a more primitive form of society in which the rules of morality are forgotten. In Western Europe, the loss of literature and culture during the Dark Ages (strictly the period between 550CE to 800CE) was brought about by excessive religious fanaticism that emptied the cities and filled the countryside with monasteries and nunneries. Whole legions of soldiers retreated into monasteries in Italy leaving it open to invasion by barbarians, as Gibbon points out. People ceased to care about humanity or its future and they lived only to serve a pitiless, non-existent entity that does nothing for us. Thus, religion regresses and demeans us when it is pursued fanatically and mindlessly. It is potentially dangerous unless it takes its proper place in the context of humanity as a whole.

There is no substitute for self-belief. Belief in our future is essential to our survival as a species. Nothing outside ourselves in any way guarantees our future. However, it is arguable that our inner resources are strong enough to ensure our future, barring unforeseeable natural catastrophes coming from comets, solar flares and the like. This book begins the task of demonstrating the strength of these resources. Thus, there is no need for faith in God, aliens, angels or whatever, as our faith in ourselves and our future is all that we require. We can go beyond ourselves without invoking supernatural presences. Contributing to posterity gives us goals that serve the future instead of the dead past as in the case of religion. Also, in section five below, it is argued that we contribute to the Cosmos in our making sense of ourselves and our environment.

We have no choice but to take responsibility for ourselves since there is no concrete evidence of anything else in the universe that has the slightest regard for us. This is not a depressing fact but a challenge to us to justify our existence against all the odds. We can easily think ourselves into extinction, never mind all the external and internal threats to our future. Indeed, it is now fashionable to doubt that humanity has any future at all. We could exterminate ourselves by self-inflicted means such as diseases concocted by deluded scientists or a nuclear war precipitated by economic collapse or by conflicts over ever-diminishing resources. There are also lots of external threats that will do the business. We could be wiped out entirely by pandemics, comets, solar radiation or whatever our fertile imaginations can conjure up.

Because all civilisations in the past have collapsed sooner or later, it is often assumed that ours is bound to follow suit. However, as is argued above, past civilisations were localised whereas ours now spans the globe. It is arguable that as the world civilisation develops and strengthens through globalisation, it is equipped better than ever to deal with local collapses and catastrophes. If Europe, America and Asia were to collapse economically, parts of Africa and Australasia may still survive the cataclysm and slowly revive the world economy.

Certainly, if we wait long enough any number of catastrophes could befall us. However, our survival as a species depends on self-belief. Once we stop believing in ourselves and our future, we deserve to become extinct. Survival means fighting for ourselves and this means finding reasons for our existence on this planet. We need to continually seek such reasons to reassure ourselves about our mission. Thus, our survival depends on finding reasons to survive and on staving off negative thinking to the contrary.

One of the biggest threats to our future at this time is a looming financial collapse due to unsustainable levels of debt throughout the world. An increased unity of nations and a reduction of national sovereignty seem necessary to organise the financial structure and eliminate debts. There is bound to be a rational solution if we work hard enough to find it. But an irrational response might result if we allow nations and organisations to compete and impose their own solutions on each other. This could lead to conflict, war and possible nuclear annihilation. Another rational alternative is for us to populate the moon and other planets, and use their resources including gold and silver to pay off our debts. These rational alternatives will be overlooked unless we response to our problems as a co-operative, unified and purposeful species. In short, we need to believe in our future as a unified species. Thus, we can only drive home the imperative need to achieve such a unity of purpose and direction for all humanity.

Belief in Humanity is not a Religious Belief.

Believing in humanity does not mean worshipping it or putting it on a pedestal. It is a matter of taking a realistic view of what we are and what we can do together. We serve humanity in acting together for the benefit of everyone. As individuals, we serve humanity by being ourselves and by behaving ourselves. This means doing the best we can and being on our best behaviour at all times since posterity is always on the watch for us.

Our belief in ourselves is not sacrosanct but must be continually justified by our meaningful thoughts and actions. Our self-belief is subordinate to our understanding of ourselves and not *vice versa* as in the case of religious belief, which makes us believe that we are the image of God. This flatters us unduly. Studying ourselves is the way forward. The more we understand about the human condition the more we have concrete and realistic grounds for believing in what we are or are not as individuals and as a species. We do not believe in ourselves absolutely but only self-critically.

The existence of a being remotely beyond and different from us cannot be understood without losing ourselves in vain fantasies and imaginings that corrupt our intellect and hence our morals. If god belief is absolute and uncritical, we can believe anything we like since we assume that whatever occurs to us intuitively comes from God rather than from our unconscious selfish desires. Killing unbelievers is the logical consequence of such absolute god belief. The humanist approach stresses the importance of starting from ourselves outward rather than starting from something outside ourselves that can only be imagined to exist.

The holistic view can bring us together. Holism is a philosophy to be understood rather than a religion to be adhered to. It is basic enough to be common to all humanity regardless of their religious beliefs or the lack of them. It constitutes a means of unifying humanity to ensure its future. To that end, it is necessary to transcend all viewpoints that divide us from each other. These viewpoints include the sectarian, national, racial, and religious divisions that set us against each other when they are treated as being more important than the interests of humanity as a whole. In this way, the holistic view contributes towards the cosmos and ultimately to cosmic unity as is argued in section five below.

The Importance of Humanity.

Many people scoff at the thought that humanity has any importance whatsoever. But they only choose to believe that we are unimportant. They may argue that way as much as they like but arguing does not make it so. The evidence can be interpreted as much from one viewpoint as from the opposite one. Such detractors are over-impressed by our astronomical insignificance in the face of an unimaginably huge universe. As regards the human condition, we can be in two minds on the matter and, like Hamlet, regard ourselves as 'the beauty of the world, the paragon of animals' and at the same time nought but a 'quintessence of dust'. The correct attitude surely is to take account of both views – both the pessimistic and optimistic views of our future. Total pessimism can't be right and complete optimism can't be either. We necessarily oscillate between the two extremes while making the best of the present. It is not certain whether the human race has a future or not but we can carry on regardless in the expectation of better things to come. Nevertheless, believing in future possibilities is all important.

The fact is that humanity is only as important as we believe it to be. Our self-belief as a species depends on our interpretation of the facts. If a person takes the pessimistic view too seriously then all the facts are inevitably interpreted from that point of view. The balanced view avoids such lop-sided thinking. The individual's life is only as trivial as they think it to be. But thinking does not make it so. It is only an opinion based on the facts. The same facts can be interpreted equally well in the other direction and used to support the opinion that one's life is not trivial. A balanced look at the facts is attempted in this book.

Some ways in which we are important. It is argued here that humanity's primary mission is to make more of the universe than has been hitherto possible by living beings. That mission is primary in the sense that it is the default position from which we can define our role on this planet. If we don't do anything else as a species we will have justified our existence. We are important in that respect because, as far as we know at this time, we alone are capable of doing this. In particular, we are also important at least in the following respects:

➢ We are important also because we are now responsible for the future of this planet and all the life-forms on it. No other species on Earth is competent to take on that role though we are ourselves diffident about taking on that role. We need to be much more organised in our handling of the planet and that entails much greater political integration and a greater purposefulness in what we do.

➤   We are important because we are increasingly unified as a species so that we can now communicate instantaneously with each other across the globe in a clear and unambiguous way that no other species can rival. This unity is spoilt by the national, religious, economic and language divisions which limit the extent to which we can communicate information.

➤   We are important as we are responsible for the next stage of evolution, namely, the machine age in which computers become increasingly intelligent and possibly self-regarding. We must be prepared to control of this situation and make sure that the value and importance of biological life is not overwritten by this development.

➤   We are important because we are the medial species between the very small and very large aspects of the universe. We are thus in a sense still at the centre of the universe even though it does not revolve around us. Our importance therefore lies in knowing that we are thus placed and in the increasing knowledge that we are acquiring about the very large and small aspects of the universe. (See pages 52-53 below for more on this)

➤   We are important because we bring value, meaning and purpose into being that does not exist otherwise. As far as we know nothing else in the universe can find any value, meaning, or purpose in it to the extent that we are doing in making sense of the universe and everything in it.

➤   We are important because we can put ourselves into context and thereby see our faults as well as our good points. We can use contexts to humble ourselves as well as elevate ourselves, but it is only by putting things into context in a practised way that we can arrive at a realistic view of what we are and what we can do.

➤   We are important because our quest for knowledge and understanding contributes to the cosmos, which consists in the continuous ordering of the universe and the consolidation of its contents, as is mentioned in section five below concerning the cosmos, cosmic unity and role of the holistic view in bringing it all together.

➤   We are important in that we are responsible for ensuring that there is a posterity which will be capable of looking back and seeing what we have or have not done for their benefit.

The Need for a Creed.

Inevitably our beliefs depend on the culture we are born into. However, as free individuals, we have the right to think out our beliefs for ourselves, regardless of the beliefs inculcated into us by the dominant culture. This means that we need not succumb to the precepts of tradition or authority without thinking them through for ourselves. Clearly, it is better for us to understand before we believe rather than to believe before understanding. In other words, we find reason within ourselves to arrive at beliefs and don't just believe something simply because we are told that it must be believed as it is god-given scripture or whatever. In this way, we give a meaning to our lives that is specifically our own.

As the meaning of our lives lies in what we make of them, we can develop that meaning by drawing on our inner resources. To become responsible for our own beliefs and opinions, we need strength of character sufficient to take on that responsibility. We should be spirited enough to enjoy thinking for ourselves. A developed inner being can access our knowledge and experiences as a whole. Compared with this holistic approach, religion has only a therapeutic value in helping people to cope with their lives in the small scale so that they cease to think critically about life as a whole. It is a retrenchment exercise that does not help any of us in seeking truths of value to the future of humanity.

The truths about humanity can be striven for interactively with an open mind. We look forward to sorting our problems out instead of looking backwardly for divine assistance. Such a human-centred view fosters our positive-mindedness and impels us to get things done rather than dwell dismally on the past. We are concerned to seek the truth and face up to it, however unpleasant or inconvenient it turns out to be. Seeking the truth is not meant to be easy but it can be an exciting and enthralling challenge, provided we have enough depth and breadth of spirit to see it as such. In this way we can keep our minds open to truthful insights.

Our future both as individuals and as a species depends on our believing in ourselves but only in a qualified and self-critical way, in other words, in a self-reflective way. We must constantly examine and re-examine our self-belief so that we can move forward and fulfil our goals and purposes in life. To that end, we need a stable, all-embracing creed based on that self-belief. Without such a creed, we have no standpoint from which to evaluate our actions, aims and purposes. Thus, such a creed can help us to be self-critical instead of forbidding criticism.

A basic creed that we can live by should be practical, sensible and down-to-earth and give us confidence in what we are as mere human beings and in what we can do collectively as a species. It should help us to do things rather than just accept things as they are. We need to think positively about ourselves and our prospects so that we can move on and embrace the future with confidence rather than dwelling on past failings and disappointments.

The characteristics of such a Creed. Thus, the need for a basic and fundamental creed may be fulfilled if it is universal enough to have characteristics such as the following:

❖   It can be embraced by all believers without necessarily threatening particular beliefs. It will add to these beliefs and not undermine them.

❖   It will go beyond all previous religious creeds while being practical, sensible and down-to-earth. It will not add to the superstitions and implausibilities to which new religions are prone.

❖   It should give us confidence in what we are as mere human beings and in what we can do collectively as a species. We need to think positively about ourselves and our prospects so that we can move on and embrace the future with confidence rather than dwelling on past failings and disappointments.

❖   It should therefore help us to do things rather than just accept things as they are. In that respect it will differ from religious creeds which typically promote passivity and obedience.

The Optimist's Creed below goes as far as possible towards fulfilling these conditions. Moreover, it does not expect any more from us than what we normally do in making something of our lives. It involves having faith in ourselves, in humanity and in power of human reason. But this faith needs constant reinforcement by our understanding and criticising what it means and how valid and applicable it is in our daily lives. In that respect, it has a practical and educational role to play rather than a ritualistic role. For the optimist would rather teach than preach, and not tell people *what* to think but *how* to think. None of the beliefs in this Creed are the whole truth of the matter, but they can help each of us to strive towards the truth in our own way. They are not themselves the way but they attempt to illuminate our way. Thus, the Creed below is a teaching tool designed to help people on their way and not to dictate what that way should be.

The Optimist's Creed helps us in our daily lives to have confidence in our place in the world, in the power of reason, in the value of our fellow human beings, and in value of life in all its varieties. It is meant to be practical and useful. It aims to make sense of matters that will chime with most people. In contrast, religious beliefs, such as a belief in the resurrection of Jesus Christ, or in the words of some long dead prophet, are not generally accepted. To that extent, they are divisive and therefore socially impractical. This Creed is intended to be the minimal belief system that can apply to us no matter what other beliefs, religious or non-religious that we may espouse over and above these beliefs. Thus, the faith of an optimist is summed up as follows:

The Optimist's Creed
The Strength of Knowledge

My faith in life and humanity is mighty because it is open-ended and founded on ever-increasing knowledge and understanding of what I am, what other people mean to me, and what life and the universe mean to me.

The Power of Critical Reasoning

I have faith in the power of critical reasoning to reach truth, foster goodness, and support justice, and I will conduct a personal quest for all these and will settle for nothing less. I will constantly strive to understand life's mysteries, as far as humanly possible, and will not be content with myths, absurdities, or similar fruitless deviations from truth. I will search for the good within me and within others and will fight for justice and sweet reason for as long as I have the strength and will to do so.

The Capabilities of Humanity

I have faith in the capabilities of humanity, notwithstanding its obvious fallibilities. My belief in its future is not unqualified, as it depends on humanity doing enough to ensure that future. If no one believes in its future then it has no future.

The Resilience of the Human Spirit

I have faith in the resilience and persistence of the human spirit which has already accomplished so much against all the odds. I believe that the spirit within us will prosper for as long as we nurture it and make the most of its potential for good and well-being.

The Uniqueness of Each Individual

I have faith in the potential of every human being to enrich the world with the uniqueness and originality of their contributions to it. I wish to see that uniqueness blossom forth in the right social conditions and thereby justify the existence of humanity.

The Possibilities of Life

I have faith in the possibilities of life which are limited only by the paucity of human imagination. I believe that life has secure foundations while the human race believes in itself and its mission to further life. This requires each of us to make the most of our lives within the limits of our unique potential. In so doing, we serve the purposes of life as much as we are the custodians of it.

Finally, humanity is like a ship at sea forever repairing itself as it sails along without being able to reach dry land where more complete and effective repairs can be made. In other words, we are a self-sustaining, self-justifying species, which must rely on its own resources and ingenuity, and can expect no external help in its endeavours. This isolation gives us opportunities and challenges that we cannot shun without dishonouring ourselves. And there is no need for us to invent friendly, helpful entities of whose existence there is no convincing evidence. If we have enough confidence in ourselves then we can do without them. When we take responsibility for our own future, they become superfluous and subject to Occam's razor.

3. Believing in the Future

The Third Principle of Prospectivism

Believing in life and humanity involves a prospective view that entails believing in the possibilities of the future and in the need to serve posterity.

The Nature of Prospectivism

Belief in the future underlies *prospectivism*. This creed consists in believing that life and humanity have a future in this universe. We may not know exactly what that future holds for us but nevertheless we can do what we can in the present to ensure that future and to make it better for purposes of posterity. The word 'prospective' comes from the Latin 'prospectus' which is the past participle of 'prospicere' – 'to look forward' or 'to look into the distance'.[8] The prospective view is relatively new since it is more natural for us to live in the past and not think too much of the future since it is fraught with uncertainties.

Only a stable and relatively dependable society, such as we are now living in, can enable us to look to the future in any confidence that it will pan out as we expect it to do. Thus, we act as *prospectivists* when we look forward to the future whereas we are *retrospectivists* when we dwell in the past and despise the future. Retrospectivists include those monks and nuns who live cloistered in the past, rock'n'rollers who live rooted in the fifties and sixties, and anyone who would rather live in the past or in some legendary Golden Age. In contrast, prospectivists appreciate the past only as a gateway to the future. We learn from it, not dwell in it.

Looking to the future is a *prospective* viewpoint, and looking to the past is a *retrospective* viewpoint. This distinction was first made by H.G. Wells in a lecture in the Royal Institution in 1902, subsequently published as *The Discovery of the Future.* He distinguished two attitudes of mind: the backward-looking 'legal mind', and the forward-looking 'creative mind'. Many people have the first attitude of mind and scarcely think of the future at all. He thought that the more 'modern' view is the latter view which "is constructive in habit, it interprets the things of the present and gives value to this and that, entirely in relation to the things designed or foreseen." However, he acknowledged that "the great mass of people occupy an intermediate position between these extremes."

The role of the prospective and retrospective viewpoints. The prospective view is optimistic about the future and the retrospective view is pessimistic about the future. For a balanced point of view, we need both of these outlooks so that the one is balanced in relation to the other. Until the modern period, the human race was overwhelmingly retrospectivist in its outlook. It is not natural for us to look too much to the future since we can be fearful of what the future has in store for us. Thus, retrospectivism is the default position to which we all revert unless we consciously adopt a prospective view. We are all retrospectivists to some extent when we immerse ourselves in the past and make too much of it. But if we want to make the most of our lives, we need to be prospective and make use of our retrospective tendencies to balance them with our prospective ones. In recent centuries, we have become more accustomed to looking forward to the future with pleasure and anticipation instead of fear and apprehension. We learn to do this with thought and experience. We are born into the present and have little apprehension of the future being any different from the past. We learn to anticipate changes in the future and the settled and predictable conditions of modern culture make us more secure about future prospects.

Thus, prospectivists use the past for future purposes, rather than looking back to the past as an end in itself. They look at the changes brought about through time, and use an understanding of past events to anticipate something different in the future. The strength of the prospectivist's vision is such that the future is looked forward to, whereas the retrospective thinker is too pre-occupied with the past to waste time speculating about the future. Studying history helps us to avoid repeating the mistakes of the past. We learn from history but we need not dwell on it. We don't need to go back and relive the past as if it were *ipso facto* better than the present. We can enjoyably relive past lives such that of Samuel Pepys in his diary but in so doing we learn how things were different in the past but the same in some ways and no better overall. People's lives in the past could be just as full and complex as our lives but in different ways.

As ever, the extremes of these outlooks are to be avoided. We keep posterity in perspective by also being retrospectivists who value the contribution of the past, but only to the extent that it can be used for future benefit. Extreme prospectivism is to be avoided as much as extreme retrospectivism. An extreme prospective view consists in our leaving everything be sorted out in the future. It leads us to do nothing for ourselves in the present. It tells us to let posterity take care of all the problems being created now. Thus, the extreme prospectivist also believes in the inevitability of human progress which will occur whatever we do in the present. Auguste Comte adopted such an extreme prospective view in his positivism that saw progress as being inevitable, while at the same time adopting an extreme retrospectivist view in respect of his religious doctrines which re-invented Catholicism in the guise of humanism.

However, even prospectivists must be unsure whether there will be a posterity. As prospectivists, we believe in the possibility of posterity rather than its actuality. The very doubtfulness of its future existence is a spur to us to do our utmost to ensure that it comes into being in the future. It all depends on us and what we do now. We must also recognise that on the one hand posterity could be much greater than we can possibly think and on the other hand it may not come to anything at all. It can go either way or none at all. The very uncertainty is necessary to ensure that we are not complacent about the future. Thus, not to be unsure about such future prospects is an extreme form of prospectivism that makes too much of the future.

Extreme retrospectivists see the future as being worse than the past. When we are not being prospectivists, then we are retrospectivists who look to the past with more favour than to the future. For those stuck entirely in an extreme retrospective outlook, the past remains a golden age that will never be surpassed in the future. Indeed, extreme retrospectivists believe that things will always get worse in the future. They dwell too much on the failings and faults that they see around them and underestimate the extent to which past achievements are being surpassed by what is happening now. For example, the importance of adhering to religious faith is exaggerated in the minds of retrospectivists because of the authority of past tradition. They have difficulty in thinking themselves out of the dictates of the past thinking to embrace the possibility of change in the future.

Whereas the extreme retrospective view dwells completely in the past, the prospective view aims to bring the past to the attention of future generations. The latter view is inclusive of all the achievements of humanity including religion. Prospectivists think about these things in relation to their future reception rather than simply recreating the past. They look forward to better things rather than looking to the past as always being preferable to the present or the future. When organisations such as the Roman Catholic Church resist changes, they are often being retrospective in their view. They tend to recreate the past in the present without thinking of the future as being any different, let alone better. The prospectivist thinks about how future generations would benefit from knowing about Catholicism - its merits as well as its faults. Thus, in this view, the study of religion is more a matter of contemplation than of rigid adherence and unquestioned devotion. Extreme retrospectivism is monistic in outlook in so far as it sees everything as one unchanging thing. The writer of *Ecclesiastes* in the Bible was a retrospectivist for whom 'there is nothing new under the sun'. Considering all the novel accomplishments of modern civilisation, it is difficult nowadays to argue that nothing new is being created that did not exist before. For example, it is a new thing to write book like this on a computer without using a pen or a typewriter.

Applying the Prospective View.

Prospectivism aspires to be the best overall belief system available to humanity. It is a post religious belief system that embraces all other belief systems, since it provides the conceptual framework within which they may all be studied, contemplated and put in their rightful place in the overall canon of human thought. Prospectivism goes beyond religion in looking forward to the future whereas religion tends to look back to the past. It is for the future of humanity in three senses: (1) it points to the future; (2) it is the future which embraces all religion; (3) it gives the human race a future to look forward to.

Prospectivism is a scientific and rational belief system that makes sense of religion in so far we can make sense of it. It is scientific in being falsifiable and the subject of constant doubt. We can never say that it is true since we are constantly doubtful whether the human race will make it in the future. As already pointed out, that very doubt encourages us to do our utmost to ensure its future. Also, we can evaluate our present activities in terms of what they may mean to future generations. Thus, a system of evaluation is possible by which prospective judgments may be made concerning the future consequences of our actions.

Prospectivism is the view that we should look to the future and think of the benefits to posterity of everything that we do. It sees the value and meaning of our deeds in their making for a better future and thus contributing to the possibility of posterity in the future. This view was first aired in the last chapter of my first book, *The Answers Lie Within Us.*

There are obvious limits to the prospective view in that we cannot live our lives worrying about what may not happen. During the Cold War period, when a nuclear Armageddon was a distinct possibility, most people went about their daily business hardly giving it a thought. And we were proved right to do so, since nothing came of these remote fears. Even during the Cuban missile crisis of 1962, when there was a real threat of nuclear war, there was no panic in the streets as most people didn't want to believe that war was impending. These days, there is probably more chance of a nuclear attack from malignant terrorists than there was then. But once again people don't want to dwell too much on such possibilities.

Only by having the courage to believe in our future can we ensure that we do have a future. People nowadays are even less rosy and optimistic about our future prospects than in Wells's day. Clearly, the human race needs to work very hard to ensure its place in the future, in view of its environmental destructiveness and the endless possibility of catastrophes such as comets, volcanoes, plagues, and wars spoiling our promising future. Nevertheless, we have to believe in the future prospects of the human race before these prospects can be realised.

The good of civilisation requires that people look as much to the future as to the past. We must think about what will be better in the future and what will benefit future generations. The study of the future ought now to be pursued just as rigorously as the study of the past. And the latter study ought to be in the service of the former one. Our greatness as a species lies in what we are about to make of the opportunities before us. It does not lie in our feeble and uncoordinated actions in the past. It consists in what is to come and in our present efforts to ensure that things are better in the future. Everything happening in the past has been, as Wells said, "but the twilight before the dawn" and past accomplishments have been "but the dream before the awakening." Our future thus consists in looking to the future, and this book attempts to work out that viewpoint as consistently as possible. Wells summed up our future prospects as follows:

> We are creatures of the twilight. But it is out of our race and lineage that minds will spring, that will reach back to us in our littleness to know us better than we know ourselves, and that will reach forward fearlessly to comprehend this future that defeats our eyes.

The Perspective of Posterity

The perspective of posterity helps us to think about our future. When we think about the future consequences of what we are doing, this is best done from that viewpoint. The ultimate service that we can perform is that which benefits posterity. Posterity is either future generations or intelligent beings in the future who are capable of understanding us. The word 'posterity' refers to 'future or succeeding generations' and 'all of one's descendants'. It comes from the Latin *posteritas* meaning 'future generations', and from *posterus* or 'coming after'. By thinking about future generations we put ourselves in their shoes and see ourselves from their point of view. We must imagine that our lives become accessible to them so that they can judge us and our lives whether we like it or not. Thus, the idea of serving posterity gives us a powerful tool by which we can evaluate the importance or non-importance of what we are doing now.

The word 'posterity' is used here not only to comprise the generations and life-forms that succeed us in the future, it also refers to what we make of the future by planning to make it better than the past. For we increase our value as individuals by serving posterity. The very meaning of our existence is enhanced as much by what we imagine that posterity will make of our existence as by what we actually make of our lives. This enhancement results from our having entered the context of posterity as well as by our anticipating how posterity may judge our present actions. In other words, we are elevated into a higher perspective of our lives by contemplating posterity. We can then think of our most mundane activities as serving posterity even when we have decided to do nothing when doing something might have adverse consequences. Serving posterity therefore means that everything we do has consequences for posterity, whether for good or ill. Whether we like it or not, we are either serving the needs of posterity or not serving its needs in whatever we do. Our judgments should always have posterity in mind; the possibility of posterity cannot be overlooked, as it is the ultimate vindication of all our efforts.

In this context the word posterity refers to future consequences and what we make of the future in the present. For our present actions have meaning for posterity whether we are aware of it or not. Making ourselves aware of posterity means bringing future generations to mind who will have to live with the consequences of what we do in the present. Future generations are important to us because everything we do now has some consequence to posterity. All our rational and purposeful activities gravitate towards the context of posterity within which the value of those activities is ultimately assessed, whether we like it or not. Everything that we do now, at this very moment, has some future meaning which cannot be ascertained in the present. We must pass on to posterity the ultimate task of judging what we do in the present. All we can do now is try to put ourselves in their shoes and make the best judgments we can.

We mostly give little thought to posterity. Yet the fact is that all our everyday actions have consequences for posterity. Every meaningful thing that we do means something for posterity. When we do something, such as buy a new car, we do it in the immediate present but the effect of our action is in the future. The money spent on the car goes into the economy, helps to pay people's wages, supports the car industry, and so on. If the car is more fuel efficient and less polluting, it reduces our travelling expenditure and is less harmful to the climate. Thus, whatever we do, it has consequences for the future whether or not we intend that there should be consequences. Future generations will either benefit or not benefit from what we do in the present. What we do now will mean something, for good or ill, to posterity, assuming that future generations will survive in the future.

If an action is meaningful to us, it will also mean something, either the same or different, in the future. When a house is renovated, those who take over the house in the future will live with the consequences of that renovation. Any long-term benefits from what we do will benefit from posterity and this gives added meaning and value to these actions. Likewise, posterity will suffer because of our shortcomings which may have adverse effects beyond our imagination. It is thus very important to judge our actions from the perspective of posterity, which can suffer from our oversights. People in the future will think badly of us in so far as we fail to do our best for them.

Posterity is More Than an Imaginary Notion.

When we think of the future we inevitably use our imagination. But the notion of a posterity awaiting us in the future is more than just imaginary. Our use of the notion is backed up, firstly, by the evidence of evolution on this planet and, secondly, by the very real possibility of advanced species living elsewhere in the universe. If the human race autodestructs or is annihilated, other living species such as insects or rodents may evolve into intelligent beings who can peer back into the past. Also, intelligent beings are probably evolving elsewhere in the universe and they may visit the Earth in the far future, (as depicted, for example, in Spielberg's 2001 feature film, *A.I. Artificial Intelligence*). Thus, what is meant here by 'posterity' includes all these possibilities, and is not just confined to our descendants in the future. Whether posterity is composed of humans, other species, aliens, androids, or computer-generated holograms, posterity will still be interested in what we do here and now. Whether we develop or fail to develop further because of our self-destruction, they will want to know the reasons why, just as we are interested in past civilisations and why they ceased to exist. At the very least, they will want to avoid the mistakes we have made in the present.

Posterity in the form of intelligent beings elsewhere in the universe is highly probable because intelligence is a natural consequence of the complexification of the universe's contents. Material bodies organise themselves into ever more complex entities by interaction and intermixture. Eventually, entities become complex enough to have lives of their own. And by interacting with their environment, such life-forms become still more complex over time. They organise themselves into communities whose cultures complexify eventually into civilisations such as our own. Cultures of sufficient complexity will produce intelligent participants, and we can expect intelligence to emerge wherever life produces complex, social beings. As there are billions of galaxies in the universe with billions of stars in each of them, the chances are that there are millions of civilisations throughout the universe. Many planets are now by being discovered that could possess forms on life. Thus, the existence of posterity in some form seems to be just as assured as the existence of any form of life in the universe.

We must work to ensure a future posterity. However, all we can do at present to ensure that there is a posterity is by working to benefit the future of humanity. We cannot afford to sit back and wait for an alien intelligent species to arrive and take our place in the cosmos. Just as parents invest their time and energy in ensuring a future for their children, so we as a species must invest all our resources in our future prospects because our descendants depend on it. Ultimately we serve ourselves best by serving the purposes of posterity. Only such service can save us in spite of ourselves as long as we work hard to serve posterity by doing things that benefit the future and make for a better future. This means for a start: (1) promoting the unity of humanity as suggested in the opening dedications of this book: eliminating nationalism, racism, and religious and ideological antipathies; (2) preserving life and caretakering the planet to a greater extent than at present; (3) peopling the moon, planets, stars since we must play our part in spreading life as widely as we can.

Broadly speaking, posterity is the culmination of all human ends. When we look to the far future, we enter the context of posterity. We can see nothing remaining of humanity unless we are succeeded by a viable posterity in the form of generations of people who will take humanity forward to a better future. Within that context we can make judgments about the consequences of our present actions. We must imagine what posterity will make of what we are doing in the present. The problems of society can only be solved in the future, and when we imagine them as they will appear to future generations, we consider in the context of posterity. However, our thoughts of the future may be mistaken unless we also consider them within such contexts as the universe, life and humanity. Within these contexts we can reach the most realistic view of matters by making use of our hard-earned past experiences when things have turned out contrary to our expectations. While the other contexts can also be depicted as containing all the others, depending on the circumstances in which they are used, posterity is ultimately the most important of all and the most of in need of over-containment rather than under-containment.

This view of posterity enables us to re-interpret the 'hereafter' as being the life of future generations that continues after our death. It gives us the possibility of an 'afterlife' of sorts. But this is not experienced by us in any shape or form since we no longer exist physically. We may have a kind of afterlife if people living in the future are able to reconstruct our lives and relive them for their own interest in the same way that we watch films and videos today about past events. We live on potentially only in so far as our lives are accessible to posterity. But this is only our lives as we have lived them in their past. They may relive our lives only in so far as their knowledge and technology allows them to do. They are unlikely to become us in merely re-running our lives as they will be unable to interfere with the things that we have already done in their past. But we can imagine that posterity is watching us as is now argued.

The Omnipresence of Posterity

As CCTV cameras are everywhere these days, it is easier than ever to imagine that we are always being watched. We might also imagine that we are constantly under the scrutiny of posterity. People or intelligent beings in the future may well have the technology to reconstruct the past and observe us in our most intimate acts and perhaps also experience what we are experiencing from one moment to the next. The assumption is that posterity is with us here and now in the sense of their knowing what we are and what we are doing just as historians know from diaries and journals what the writers were feeling and what they were doing at a certain time in the past.

The presence of posterity is not a physical, or even a ghostly or supernatural, presence. Unless time travel becomes a real possibility, people living in the future are here with us only in having access to knowledge about what we were doing at a certain point in their past. In that way they are able to reconstruct in visual form, by means of an advanced 'virtual reality', the scenes and events in which we ourselves are living our lives at this very moment. The events we are presently experiencing may be imprinted and recorded in the atoms and molecules of our bodies, the air, floor, walls, furniture, and so on. Our lives may also be recorded in some way at the quantum level of existence.

We can imagine that their technology will enable them to reconstruct these recorded events from the atoms and molecules that were formerly in our bodies, the air, and so on. Perhaps they will virtually get inside our skins and feel and think what we are feeling and thinking, here and now. But they will only do so in the future and they cannot change events here and now. They will not be able to make us feel and think things or to influence us into doing anything other than what we are actually doing at the present time.

The notion of a superior being who is with us all the time and everywhere only makes sense as a way of heralding the scarcely imaginable abilities of posterity to reconstruct the past and to understand present events better than we do ourselves who are living through them. Thus, we can look forward to posterity having the possible cognisance of our most intimate thoughts and acts. 'Heaven' is what posterity has in store for us in making life even more meaningful than it seems to be during our own lifetime. This kind of heaven may seem fantastical, but it is a real possibility nevertheless. Though a person's life might seem meaningless in present day terms, it is perfectly possible that it will be much more meaningful to posterity in the far future, assuming that intelligent life of some kind does survive into the far future.

Thus, instead of the ubiquity of God, we should consider the ubiquitous vigilance of posterity. The idea of our acts being subject to perpetual surveillance has been recognised since the earliest times. For example, in the dialogue, *Phaedrus*, Socrates warns the lusty youth beside him that the cicadas in the surrounding trees are witnesses to whatever deeds they observe and that they report their findings directly to the Muses. A consciousness of unknown and unseen witnesses to our most intimate acts has been with us since we developed the imagination to think of things not really being what they are immediately perceived to be. Thus, gods, spirits, demons, and angels were posited as possible witnesses of everything we do. Having a better developed scientific imagination than our ancestors, we can now assign this possibility to the future where the ability to reconstruct the past will be a distinct possibility, given the requisite theoretical knowledge and technological know-how.

The Great Day of Judgment awaits us all in posterity wherein we will all be judged according to whatever we have or have not done in our lives. We may not be personally called before the tribunal of posterity to account for our failings, but our lives will be. In leaving these lives behind us to be judged by in the future, we can never be sure how they will be judged. All we can be sure of is that enough traces will be left behind of our having lived, and of how we lived, to enable these lives to be evaluated one way or another. Therefore, posterity will judge us whether we like it or not. We are all 'doomed' in that respect. On the other hand, the thought of being watched all the time doesn't necessarily change our behaviour. The Big Brother television series shows that even though people know that they are being observed 24 hours a day with television cameras, that knowledge does not stop them from making fools of themselves. However, they are admittedly paid to do so for the entertainment of the public.

Our *nunc stans* or everlasting 'now' means that what happens right 'now' belongs to the universe as a whole. All our 'nows' are shared with every other event in the universe and are inextricably linked to them. Everything we experience in the present is a permanent contribution to the cosmos available for all time to come. The 'now' consists in a second to second confrontation with the potential choices which we use our freewill to actualise by means of our mental and physical activities. There is no need to contemplate survival after death as each 'now' lasts forever as it passes into the past where everything is preserved for the potential purposes of posterity.

Even dying completely alone and unknown to the rest of humanity will not allow us to escape the tribunal of posterity, since everyone living and everything happening in the present will be known about in the future. Advanced beings in the future, by virtue of being more advanced, will have better technological means by which to study the past than archaeologists have today in their examining the past of human beings. Everything that is happening here and now can be reconstructed in the future as long as the technological problems can be overcome by finding out how to do it. We lack such a technology now and we can barely imagine how it can be done but our descendants in the distant future may well acquire it. If we take our lives seriously then we must act on the assumption that they will do so.

But, as already suggested, these advanced beings are unlikely to have the power to interfere with and change the lives of intelligent beings in the present. Unless they physically travel back into the past, they will be unable to interfere with the freewill of intelligent beings because the physical impossibility of reaching into the past and altering events. Time travel may prove to be impossible because the inexorable expansion of the universe into the future precludes the possibility of changing the past in any physical way. Such beings could have greater power over the universe as a whole than over individual intelligent beings in the past. Our capacities are presently actualised only in the small scale but superior beings in the future may have technological command of the whole universe's workings.

We can speculate about the godlike abilities of superior beings without believing in their actual existence. More advanced entities than intelligent beings might be more spiritual than material, as anticipated in the form of 'angels' by scholastic philosophers such as Aquinas. Complete spirituality implies being involved totally in potentialities at the expense of actualities. Their lives would revolve round potentialities without the need to actualise them in physical terms. They could create and destroy the potentialities that we are able in our finite world to choose between and exercise our freewill in doing so.

The function of advanced entities in the universe might therefore be that of manipulating potentialities so that some are more available to be actualised than others. They would be responsible for those coincidences and other events that seem to be more than just the product of random chance. If this is the case, then lucky and unlucky individuals are in the hands not of the gods but of these more advanced and wholly potential beings in the future. This activity would not threaten the freewill of intelligent beings as it does not affect their mental or physical activities but only the range of possibilities with which they are confronted. Thus, more advanced beings might have an influence over chaotic events, but not over the organised, complex decision-making of lesser beings such as ourselves.

The ultimate goal of these advanced beings could be the perfecting of the universe by manipulating potentialities. This would mean creating the mechanisms that are increasingly better at producing intelligent beings and at giving them a chance of a better and more fortunate life. However, this may not have relevance to the present universe; it may only apply to future universes that are spawned out of the present one.

If these beings do have any influence over present potentialities then there is a feedback operation involved here. It means that in benefiting posterity, intelligent beings are improving the ability of advanced entities to make more good luck and fortune available for intelligent beings in the present. In spite of the fact that good and bad luck have a random and ultimately unpredictable element because of the randomness of quantum wave/particle events, this does not necessarily preclude an element of good and bad luck that is 'caused' by events taking place in the distant future and by technological means beyond present conceptions.

This suggests that, in not doing his best to fulfil his potentialities, the intelligent being diminishes the future potentialities of the universe as a whole. His failure has a knock-on effect on his own life as it makes him less 'lucky'. His good luck is liable to run out since it relies on a conjunction of events that are outside his own control. But some of these events may be in the potential control of more advanced beings in the future. The welfare of these beings may depend on their lives being as productively beneficial to the universe as possible. The good things done in the life of an intelligent being will benefit these beings and give them greater potential to control the conjunction of events in his favour.

The ultimate destiny of the universe may therefore lie in what it bequeaths to eternity to justify its existence. The fate of everything that happens in the universe depends on these events being an indelible part of eternity so that they might not have occurred in vain. Science in the far distant future may have the task of ensuring either that the universe continues indefinitely with its contents intact or that its contents are bequeathed to another universe spawning from it.

There are doubtless more reasons than are presently available why intelligent beings are gaining such extensive knowledge and control of the universe. If there is not more to be understood, it must be asked, how could such a possibility be even comprehended, let alone put into words or symbols which other intelligent beings might understand? The very possibility of gaining such understanding itself seems to be part of the fabric of the universe. In a sense, it is there waiting to be found, even though, in another sense, we are making it up as we go along. The ambiguity arises because we have to discover it for ourselves in our own terms that are personal to us. Thus, we and all other intelligent beings strive for this better understanding of the universe and our part in it, perhaps for no better reason than that this task is there to be done and that we are capable of doing it.

Part Two
The Purpose of Belief

4. Serving Life and Humanity

The Fourth Principle of Prospectivism
A belief in life and humanity requires us also to serve life and humanity to the best of our abilities since it is only in that service they will have a future worth living. We serve ourselves as much as we serve others when there are clear mutual benefits.

Service is the purest form of love. At its best, it is untrammelled by personal, let alone sexual, motivations. When it is focused exclusively on the welfare and wellbeing of the object of one's service, it can't be bettered. In doing useful things for each other, we demonstrate the extent of our regard for each other. We thereby serve ourselves, and make more of ourselves by making more of others. Yet it is not always necessary to be doing things to serve people – "They also serve who only stand and wait" – as Milton put it. In continuing to live decent lives we serve life because being a living creature is a significant thing in itself. We wake up each day with the potential to add some of value to life in itself.

We must find out for ourselves the purposes implied by our beliefs. Life itself is a process of fulfilling purposes of one kind or another. We do purposeful things in continuing to live and in making the best of our lives. In so doing we benefit others as well as ourselves. There is no point in believing in life and humanity and their future unless we are prepared to do something with these beliefs. They have a function in motivating us to change things for the better.

How we can serve life. Serving life is the highest form of service. Hence the importance of doctors, nurses and health professionals in our society; hence the importance of biologists, zoologists and all those who study and look after animals and care about them. Our interest in the welfare of animals and other life forms motivates us to serve them by looking after them.

How we can serve humanity. Serving life goes along with serving humanity. They are not antithetical. We need them both together and not in opposition to each other. If we are to work together to achieve the future aims of society, we must be prepared to serve one another. This means making ourselves useful in one capacity or another. It does not mean making an abject slave out of ourselves. Humanity must be subordinated to the individual and not the other way round which is the authoritarian way. The humanist view is that humanity must serve us as much as we serve humanity. Moreover, we are all humanists by virtue of belonging to the human race. Not to be a humanist is to be barely human, but a slave to the creeds of some dictator, priest, mullah or whatever.

Thus, as humanists our role is that of serving humanity, both as individuals and as a collective species, with a view to being served by humanity in our turn. We show how much we value other people by serving them. If we are wise we do not live for ourselves alone but enjoy serving and pleasing other people as well as ourselves. It is natural for us to commit ourselves to the service of other people. In a sense we are born to serve each other, and it is only human to make ourselves useful to each other. We normally do this quite naturally when we are getting something worthwhile in return for our servitude, for example, a good living wage. In serving other people we put them at the centre of our world but only within the limited purposes of the service we wish to perform. We start with individuals and work our way up to humanity as a whole. The individual is more important than humanity as every single human being is an indispensible part of humanity.

If we cut ourselves away entirely from other people, we risk making ourselves less than human. Being human means interacting with others to bring out our unique human traits. Our common humanity alone brings us together. It is natural for us to have fellow feelings for every human being on the planet and not allow our ideas, beliefs or opinions to diminish these feelings or lessen our view of them. The plight of each person on Earth is our common concern.

The difficulty with service lies in distinguishing it from slavery, loss of freedom and thraldom. Service is not slavery as long as we are acting from own freewill and are being treated with the dignity and respect due to every human being. In that respect, being of service to others is fulfilling and liberating. When service stops being fulfilling and liberating then it is indistinguishable from slavery. But it all depends on how we see the role ourselves. We may willingly make slaves of ourselves and not think of ourselves as slaves.

An unfortunate consequence of socialist/communist thinking is that servants and workers are seen as making slaves of themselves. According to that view, we should all be equal as working human beings. The collapse of the serving class as prominent feature in our society resulted from this mistaken point of view. People were metaphorically turned out into the streets to fend for themselves, thus creating a society of loners. The leisure class now includes poor people who live permanently on benefits. In contrast, a society in which people willingly become servants is more cohesive as people come together to live with and for each other. For example, the 17th century musketeers in Alexandre Dumas's novel *The Three Musketeers* are portrayed as having their own 'valets' who acted as servants, even though the musketeers themselves were as poverty-stricken as their servants, who were nevertheless happy in that role.

The fact is that we are not all equal human beings. We are all different and we thrive on our differences. Attempts to iron out our economic and social differences are bound to cause more grief than relief. We are all equal in being different from each other, and the fairest society maximises our opportunities to make the most of our differences without depriving anyone of their opportunities. A society based on our serving one another in one capacity or another arguably gives us all the best chance of attaining the ideal of equal opportunities for all. Too much emphasis on equality has the paradoxical effect of exacerbating competition between people as they strive to differentiate themselves in a society of undifferentiated equals. We need to work together, not against each other.

Co-operation is more important than competition. We have evolved to be a co-operative as well as a competitive species. We progress by balancing these two tendencies. But co-operation must predominate as the unity and survival of society depends more on co-operation than on competition. The balance is achieved by ensuring that we work together while competing with each other. Football teams work together to arrange matches and agree to play to the same rules in their competitions. It is therefore in their own interests to serve the same aims and thus serve one another.

Serving one another is the best way for us to co-operate towards the common ends of humanity. Our unity depends on a culture of service more than on a culture of competition. The most progressive periods in our history have been those in which service has been to the fore, even though other aspects of everyday life such as war, famine and plague might not have been so propitious. Therefore, co-operation is more important to our survival than competition. The latter only makes sense when we are vying with each other to better our service to others. The most successful organisations under capitalism are those that are more efficient in their service provision than in their profit-making. Internet companies such as Amazon and Google became successful because of the efficiency of their service and only later did they become exorbitantly profitable. The most popular organisations in the UK are the BBC and the National Health Service, neither of which make profits. Also, Wikipedia is obviously an entirely voluntary organisation whose service is universally used and appreciated.

We vindicate ourselves through serving the needs of other people, humanity and life forms in general. Our lives are thereby made more valuable to ourselves and others. Our common humanity consists in making ourselves available for such services and this makes us feel that we belong and are a part of the whole. Also, our daily lives would be impossible without the service of others when we buy goods and services, seek to be entertained and so on. It is only right and just that we should serve others in our turn. Our very survival as a species depends on our willingness to serve each other. Our civilisation would cease to exist if we all lived for ourselves alone like male orang-utans. When we know that other people are devoted to serving us honestly and to the best of their abilities, we can trust and rely on them unconditionally. Thus, service is a necessary prerequisite to trust and reliability in our social relationships.

Our security depends on other people being willing to be of service to us. For example, the idea of service to the community offers a way of tackling the problems of internet privacy, snooping, and exploitation.   We would be more confident that internet organisations are acting in our best interests if their use of internet information is shown to be strictly in our service. Our interests must be paramount in the access and use of internet information about the people's personal lives and activities. These organisations should be obliged to keep us informed and to demonstrate periodically their commitment to this prime principle of service.

Counselling of all Kinds Helps People

We can serve our fellow human beings particularly well by counselling them. This may mean no more than giving them useful advice or giving them help to understand their problems better. It can therefore be performed either professionally or personally. In the past, it was left entirely to religious people to offer counselling to people. But this is increasingly unacceptable, especially when so many priests and clergy are shown to use their profession for their own personal, prurient purposes.

The tendency of religion is to counsel its servants to keep them enslaved to its orthodox beliefs. Its fault lies in making people the means to the end of religion instead of being ends in themselves. Religion gives comfort by offering absolute certainties. In doing so, it does not help people inside themselves. A listening counsellor is liable to be more helpful with people's problems than the canting preacher, as the psychologist, Anthony Storr noted: "If anyone is in urgent need of help or guidance, let him find someone who will listen rather than preach; someone who will encourage him to look inward and find out what he as a unique individual thinks and believes, rather than accepting some guru's dogma."

Counselling is best performed by professionals who are trained and experienced in helping people. But we can also vindicate ourselves in the counselling that we offer others in our daily lives, when they come to us in times of need. We can comfort people by assuring them of the meaningfulness of their lives. We encourage them to contemplate the astonishing gift that the life is. We give them hope by showing them the bigger picture and how everything fits together. What makes no sense in itself makes perfect sense on the whole. If all else fails, we can adopt a stoical frame of mind by which we doggedly put up with unpleasant things.

Counselling serves humanity when it genuinely helps people. It may not do so if it is imposed on them as a matter of form. Not everyone wants or needs counselling and they should have a choice in the matter. Its role is diminished if it becomes compulsory or enforceable in any way, since it no longer serves but becomes a bureaucratic imposition that interferes with freedom of choice. It then no longer serves real needs but becomes a bureaucratic imposition that interferes with freedom of choice.

In helping people, it is important to distinguish professional from personal or emotional help. Professional help is motivated by rational love that is passionate but also disinterested. It is constrained by the reasons, rules, morals, knowledge and expertise of the profession. Personal or emotional love is often based on selfish and thoughtless feelings. The tyrannical organisation or society is typically dominated by the personal feelings of the person in charge. You are required to show unqualified love and loyalty to the tyrant to retain your position in the organisation. In the Roman Empire, everyone had to show an unqualified 'love' for the Emperor. Anyone whose love was considered lacking could expect a visit from the local centurion to terminate their life processes, one way or another. Such love is akin to slavery. Professionalism in our modern society has developed to eliminate the need to enslave ourselves to people to get what we want. Our freedoms depend upon our serving society in a rational way and on society behaving rationally and respecting our rights in return.

Serving Society

We serve society and it serves us in its turn. Throughout our lives we serve society in one way or another simply by being rational people doing reasonable things. This means behaving in a friendly and sociable way on most occasions, despite provocations or adverse distractions. By being sociable people we make society more tolerable for other people. Society is after all no more than all of us interacting together to get through our daily lives as comfortably and happily as we can. But it is also useful to think of our relationship to society in formal terms. We serve society and society serves us, so that, whether we like it or not, there is a formal relationship going on which only lacks a name. Also, serving others inevitably means serving society as every human relationship is a part of society as a whole.

In so far as we submit to the two-way service of society we enter into an implicit *civic covenant.* This is not to be confused with what was called a 'social contract' which was a legalistic concept to be imposed on the individual by the authorities. The civic covenant is here seen as a matter of individual choice. We enter this covenant on becoming socially responsible persons who choose to take their place in society as free citizens. In entering this covenant, we pay for our freedoms by taking on various obligations and responsibilities. In return, society freely gives us the facilities and organisations we need in living our lives freely and responsibly. In that way, the civic covenant involves two-way obligations – a give-and-take involving both society and the individual. No money or additional services are exchanged in initiating and continuing this covenant. It is implicit and unspoken on both sides.

In giving of our best, we need to know where we stand and what is expected of us. To maintain the social structure, some basic obligations and responsibilities are implicitly laid down. For instance, the right to freedom of self-expression may accompany an obligation to marry, have children and be responsible for raising a family. Such a promotion of normal family life secures a base for the healthy flourishing of the personality.

Moreover, the civil covenant has moral rather than legal force. We enter into the civic covenant of our own freewill. It is not to be enforced by society in any legal or authoritarian manner. It is only binding on the individual's conscience as it has moral rather than legal force. The civil covenant can be taught in schools so that it becomes the product of education and social expectation. An understanding of this implicit covenant can sharpen up young people's moral sense and sensitivity in particular. Basically, it means behaving ourselves, being answerable to other people and in that way rationalise and socialise our behaviour. You are expected to behave in a sociable way and the civic covenant merely reflects that expectation. The civil covenant is only important from a legal point of view in that it obviates the need for endless prohibitive legal enactments that infringe our freedoms and turn society into a legalistic police state ruled by police, lawyers and judges. It can therefore contribute to our liberation from the restrictive legalism that is currently intruding into every part of our private lives. It does so by appealing to our moral sense and becoming a habit of thought instead of being imposed on us legally.

The civil covenant is therefore quite distinct from the age-old notion of a 'social contract'. From Hobbes onwards, this contract was a legal one in which individuals submitted to the authority of government for protection, justice and the rule of law. The civil covenant differs in being made by each individual with themselves and for themselves alone. Thus, the 'original contract' is not with groups combining for self-protection and justice (*vide* Hobbes, Locke, Hume, Rousseau, Kant, Rawls, Nozick, *et al*), but with our individual selves opting into society with all its obligations and responsibilities for our own personal purposes to reap the opportunities and benefits for oneself alone. In being part of the legal system, the social contract is imposed on people instead of being understood as being part of the way we live and take our part in society.

Anyone engaging in anti-social behaviour is not so much breaking any social covenant as putting their own selfish concerns before other people's interests. Thus, the source of anti-social behaviour can be seen in the individual's personal failings. It is not solely a matter of law-breaking but mainly a failure to see that it is in their own interests to serve society and thereby serve themselves. Terrorists, sociopaths and hardened criminals break the covenant by alienating themselves and making a personal war on society. They have lost all respect for society because they no longer see a place for themselves in it. If they are taught to see the benefits of society in the light of the social covenant, this may help to obviate their alienation. It clarifies the fact that anti-social behaviour is not in their overall interests as unique individuals having a unique role to play in society.

The civil covenant reflects that fact that moral progress comes from within and cannot be enforced by society. We make moral progress in our expectations of each other's behaviour. For instance, it is no longer acceptable to behaviour for men to ill-treat or abuse women or children, or to treat them as sex objects. Also, we are no longer allowed to give way with impunity to our feelings and impulses like animals. These expectations are learnt by people as part of their education and social upbringing. Their minds become tuned to the expectations of society and there is no need for these expectations to be enforced by fear of authority or legalistic sanctions. Moral progress is possible but only to the extent that moral self-discipline is taught and appreciated by everyone as individuals.

Serving Society Through Prospectivism

Prospectivism is a creed that has a valuable role to play in the community. The most important service that prospectivism offer society is to educate the public (1) about the value of life, (2) about living together for our common ends, and (3) about the role of intelligence and creativity in our lives. Education does not end in childhood but lasts till death.

Its educational role. First and foremost, these aims depend on the inculcation of the basic skills and facts required for living in a complex society. The skills begin with reading, writing and arithmetic but include also art and music. The facts should be learnt by stimulating people's interest in them. We must both 'fill the vessel' and 'kindle the fire' of every individual. Plutarch is often quoted inaccurately as saying that "a child's mind is not a vessel to be filled but a fire to be kindled". But it is not a case of either/or. We need both the filling and the firing. In other words, we need both discipline and freedom in our educational methods in more or less equal measures. We need the disciplined inculcation of skills and facts as well as the undirected freedom of finding out things for ourselves. The teacher should interplay both these aspects in the education process.

Filling the vessel usually precedes the kindling of the mind since it provides the basic skills and information without which the fire cannot take hold or last for long. Our minds need to be filled with skills, facts, thoughts, and memories. Skills must be inculcated, facts must be absorbed, thoughts must be stimulated in a rational way, and the memory must be trained by constant repetition. Otherwise there will be insufficient kindling to be fired, and the fire will be ineffective if the skills or knowledge are not up to the task. In other words, an ineffective education system will give people the equipment they need to take their rightful places in society.

The end of prospective education is also to train the mind to be far-seeing and comprehensive, taking the broadest possible outlook on life, experiencing more of it, and understanding more about it than otherwise. Prospectivists can strive to be *indagators* and *scrutators* – searchers for the truth and examiners of it when it is found or at least thought to be found. As indagators we are always delving deeply for the truth. As scrutators we are never wholly satisfied that the truth has indeed been found. This is only outlines the prospective approach to education.

Its pastoral role. Though it is not a religion, prospectivism has a pastoral role to play in society. It is the practical application of prospectivism that shows it to be more than an ivory tower activity. This role is directed particularly to three basic needs: the social, ethical and metaphysical.

❖   *The social need* concerns our fitting into society, finding friends and living amicably with our neighbours and workmates. We are essentially gregarious animals that are at our best among other people. Prospectivism therefore aims to help individuals to become better and more sociable persons taking that place in society which suits them and makes the best of their talents and abilities.

❖   *The ethical need* concerns our behaviour and the discipline and self-restraint we must learn to apply if we are to be useful and reliable citizens. The exercise of morality provides the tools by which a person's moral sense is strengthened and moral insights are achieved.

❖   *The metaphysical need* concerns the meaning of life and our existential angst about the value of our lives. This is catered for by the additional prospective exercises mentioned below that explore our role in the universe and what we are meant to do in the universe.

Its counselling role. As mentioned above, prospectivism fosters a caring and compassionate attitude of mind. This is achieved particularly in the exercise of service. It consists in offering succour to the weak, suffering, depressed, unhappy and needy individuals in society. Also, the exercise of vitality means reaching inwards for inner strength. This helps us to stave off the boredom, dullness, indifference, and disinterestedness from which we all suffer from time to time. Our inner reserves of emotions, knowledge and wisdom can rescue us from negative feelings and existential angst. Thus, our moods may make us feel dull and listless but we can avoid prolonged depression or even bipolar swings of mood by focusing on positive things and keeping busy. Churchill suffered greatly from his 'black dog' depressions but he fought against his nature manfully with results we are all familiar with. Many great men suffered similarly: Goethe, Schumann, Luther, Tolstoy and many others. The various exercises of prospectivism aim to give strength and encouragement in relieving such emotional impediments.

Its fellowship role. Prospectivism offers company and fellowship to all those desiring it. By social means, it aims to bring people together with the common ends of benefit each other and society as a whole. It treats the human race as an enlarged family that embraces everyone on the Scottish principle – "Wir a' Jock Tamson's bairns'. We all belong to one family, and nobody is excluded from the family of humanity because we are all the same in being human beings. Thus, there is only one admissible form of racism – human racism, as is mentioned below on pages 61-62.

Its ceremonial role. As a social and humanist organisation, it can offer the usual celebrant ceremonies associated with birth, marriage and death. Ceremonies are very useful but not in the form of repetitious rituals resonant of obsessive compulsive disorder. It will also organise celebrations of important events and of the lives of people important to the ethos of prospectivism. We can make our daily routines sacred to us in a secular way. Any prospective ceremonies are performed for their entertainment, historical or educational value and not because of any spiritual or religious significance that is inauthentic and has no basis in life or reason.

Its moralist role. This role is chiefly fulfilled by the morality exercise mentioned on page 7 above and further discussed in my book *Advancing Humanity* on pages 114-144. Also, prospectivism cannot flourish in an abnormal society that lacks moral parameters within which people are expected to behave. In a normal society, there are clear norms to which we are expected to adhere within rational limits. Thus, one of the functions of moral discourse is find reasons for and against conformity to established norms.

Its political role. Prospectivism has a political role to play in society in promoting the advancement of humanity as against any alternative that demeans people and impedes their progress. The unity of humanity means promoting and sustaining all political moves towards that unity. However, Prospectivism is not directly concerned with party politics as it considers both sides of any argument dispassionately with a view to getting things done. Democratic politics are faulty in compelling people to take sides on the right or left, on the conservative or progressive side of things. Prospectivism teaches us to understand and appreciate both sides of any position in conformity with the dualist view mentioned below on pp. 51-2.

Improving Prospective Exercises

Improving and Enhancing Prospective Exercises are also necessary to develop the prospective view. To serve effectively we need inner exercising that builds up our spiritual reserves. In that way, we can better understand our capabilities and their limits. There is more on the following topics in my book, *Advancing Humanity* (2016).

1. *Vitality* – This is the inner strength that we need to achieve self-fulfilment. The knowledge and development of our inner vitality contributes to our self-knowledge. It means developing our 'inner being' which unifies everything going on inside us. Inner being governs the strength or weakness of our so-called 'character'. Generally speaking, the stronger our character, the more developed is our inner being. Its development is the *sine qua non* of a vital and affirmative attitude to life. Sustaining this development enables us to keep going against all the odds.

2. *Illuminosity* – Light is all important to life and humanity since the light of the sun makes life possible on Earth. The light of the universe in general gives life the energy that it needs to survive and thrive. We are useless in the dark both literally and metaphorically. Likewise, the act of believing clarifies what was previously confused and unclear. It shines a light on things. Belief thus begins as an act of enlightenment in which you see the point in believing in life and humanity. What was previously unclear becomes as clear as the light of day. Thus, enlightenment clarifies things and brings forth meaning and significance that did not exist before. Our future depends on our emerging into the light of day instead of lurking in the darkness of selfishness and self-centredness.

Thus, illumination is an important starting point for making ourselves fit for the world. We can get too wrapped up in our thoughts and feelings. Our dark side can emerge all too easily and fill us with despair. For imbedded in inner being is the darkness of the soul. This darkness forever threatens to engulf us. We need to pour light on it and dispel it or at least keep it at bay. Illumination is required to counter excessive introspection and bring us into the light of love and understanding. We need to bring out what is within us so that others can see our inner worth. Otherwise we remain stunted introverts having nothing to say and little to do with ourselves. Thus, illumination is the antidote to excessive obsession with self. It is the externality that contrasts with the internality in which the vitalist can become too involved. It is the source of all will-power and self-determination and it develops over time through an intensification and unification of our experiences of life. It thereby forms the basis of one's personality, namely, that which is unique and singular about us.

3. *Creativity* – What makes humanity particularly important on this planet is our creativity. What we create in all fields of activity brings new things into being that did not exist before. We enrich the planet thereby even when we inadvertently destroy things in the process. But the more creative we become, the more we find ways to create without being so destructive of our environment. In believing in life and humanity we want to contribute to their future wellbeing. In creating something of which we are proud, we add to the sum of human achievements. We apply our beliefs by what we do to people, in society, on the Earth, everywhere and to everything.

Exploiting our creativity is essential to the future of humanity. We would have achieved little or nothing in the past without our creativity which has been our salvation and our vindication throughout the ages. But it is up to each of us to find our own creative area as this is the ultimate expression of our individuality. Creativity is one of the many 'invisible hands' by which all of us together contribute meaningfully to the whole in pursuing our self interest. Smith's 'invisible hand' referred mainly to monetary wealth accumulated by individual efforts. But the wealth of artistic creativity is surely worth more to humanity than all the gold, silver and fiat currency circulating throughout the world. Even if we had no money, we would still have art, music, literature, buildings and other means to express ourselves and find enjoyment in life.

In the widest sense, we can all be creative artists of one sort or another. We can all create things and be artists in that sense. We enrich our lives by making the most of our potential artistry. As artists, we can dream up new ideas and new ways of doing things that never been thought of or created before. If we can successfully put our dreams into practice, we give them a concrete existence that will last for as long as their materiality persists. Thus, our artistic role is to bring new things into being that will be long-lasting and ultimately eternal.

4. *Morality* – To serve life and be served by it, we need to be self-disciplined which entails self-discipline and having a moral viewpoint to live by. The past achievements of humanity have depended greatly on individuals behaving morally. This is morality in the sense of applying moral discipline; it is not avoiding sinfulness, but getting things done and making decent lives for ourselves and others. We are all sinners in the sense of being imperfect beings who make mistakes, but what matters is doing what is worthwhile in our own and other people's judgments. Totally self-indulgent individuals are unlikely to achieve great things. If we follow our

immediate feelings unreservedly and consistently, we will lack the discipline and energy to do what we ourselves really want to do. Total lack of moral restraint means killing each other when we feel like it, cheating and lying with every word we speak, having sex with each other without shame like bonono apes, and so on. We would be unable to live together and trust each other. Our social ties therefore depend on the acceptance and practice of moral behaviour.

Thus, we need morality to give us rules for our conduct and boundaries within which to behave ourselves. Without such rules and boundaries, there are no limits to the inappropriate or self-destructive behaviour to which we may stoop. By learning to live within such moral confines we can become normal, trustworthy and hardworking people. We can freely adopt and practice the norms of society and become mature and responsible people who are ready to take our place in society. Wholesomeness is necessarily incomplete without the sound moral basis that makes us life-long moralists.

Enhancing Prospective Exercises

We cannot serve life and humanity to the best of our abilities without understanding something of our place in the universe. Such understanding helps us to appreciate the importance of our role both as individuals and as a species. The unknowledgeable person is an enslaved person, subject to the whims of self-assured people who claim to be knowledgeable without justification. There is no substitute for knowing things for yourself.

The following topics of emergence, duality and centrality are to be found in more detail in my book, *The Promise of Dualism* (2016):

1. *Emergence – How life came to the fore:* We begin by using scientific knowledge to understand how life and humanity have emerged as natural products of the universe's development. We thereby understand better our place in the universe. The intimacy of our connection with the universe is made apparent and this reinforces our role in it. All our beliefs begin with the emergence of life which came forth using the natural processes of the universe. Nothing else is required; we need no supernatural or divine interventions.

Life came to the fore spontaneously and interactively. We benefit by contemplating how it has emerged from the simplest components of the universe and has been complexifying ever since. For the complexity of life and humanity is deeply embedded in the structure and development of the universe. Intelligent life has emerged from the dust of the universe just as surely as life itself, and it is doubtless doing so at this moment in the nooks and crannies of distant galaxies. A process of complexification is involved in which entities become more complex in their internal interactions.

Organic entities are more complex because of their metabolic activity and organic interactions. The variety and velocity of their interactions do not exist in inorganic entities. The latter are simpler in their structure and therefore simpler in their internal interactions.

By understanding complexification, we see how both life and humanity are products of the complexifying processes of the universe. We live in a complex universe that has been growing ever more complex over time. Since the beginnings of the universe, its parts have come together and become more complex in their internal structure. Eventually, more complex elements such as carbon were produced that made life possible. The growth and development of complexity led to the formation of life forms without which the universe alone cannot understand itself. This act of understanding is needed to bring increasing order into existence when its complexity is reduced to mathematical formulae. Thus, scientific endeavour is itself a natural product of the way the universe is complexifying itself. We are a natural culmination of this complexification process that has been producing entities of ever greater complexity until it has now reached a life-form that is capable of comprehending that complexity and doing something with it to bring greater order and unity into the universe. What complex forms lie beyond us remain to be seen.

2. *Duality – Seeking the Middle Way:* Between opposing views, there is always the possibility of a middle way. Thus, the dualist view is beneficial in preventing the polarisation of opposing and competing beliefs. Absolutism leads to such a polarisation. Absolute certainty in their beliefs encourages opponents to go to war with each other to resolve their differences once and for all. This mentality is based on a monism that centres everything on one idea, one person, one religion, or one way of thinking. It is the antithesis of the dualist view which is more relativist than absolutist. According to the dualist view, nothing can be said to be absolutely the case. There is always the possibility of doubt and uncertainty. Dualist studies show that effective action is possible because of this doubt and uncertainty and not in spite of it. The long-term effectiveness of action depends on our taking account of all factors in a dualist manner whereas the short-term solutions of politicians are a response to media inspired crises.

Dualist studies are therefore needed to correct the faulty ways of thinking that lead us (1) into extremism and absolutism in one direction or (2) into error, doubt and confusion in the other direction. In other words, we must improve the tools of human reason if we are to survive as a species and think our way out of our problems without despairing of the future. The dualist view is anti-absolutist as extremism is a major obstacle to our advancement. Extreme views create needless conflicts by the violent disagreements and enmity that they engender. The extremist mentality can be countered by showing the limited nature of the truths on which it relies. The dualist view is an essential tool in drawing attention to the limited truth of all our beliefs and opinions. There is always a lot to be said for opposing views in our quest for truth. Unless we see the limitations to our beliefs and opinions they cannot be applied to reality with any confidence. These limitations are usually defined by the context in which they can be applied with confidence. The success of scientific theories has resulted from their being applied very exactly to the situations in which they can be used with total confidence. Extremist beliefs are typically applied indiscriminately everywhere without critical examination. Thus, we need dualist studies to facilitate the search for the middle way and the avoidance of harmful extremes.

3. *Centrality – Living at the Centre of Things*

Life and humanity are immensely small compared with the immensity of the universe. Nevertheless, they are important because they occupy the middle position between the very small and the very large. The truth about our importance lies in examining exactly what science tells us our place in the universe. We are indeed insignificantly small in relation to the universe at large. But we are in our turn immensely large in relation to the miniscule atomic sphere of existence. We are a middle species that lies between the imaginably large and the inconceivably small areas of existence.

The true scale of our physical insignificance is scarcely imaginable. The Earth is not much bigger than pinhead from the distance at which the sun is positioned. The whole solar system is even smaller than a pinhead in relation to the Milky Way galaxy of which it forms a part. Our galaxy appears to be no more than a pinhead from far outside it. And there are millions upon millions of other similar tiny galaxies in the universe. We are infinitely small within infinitely small pinheads. We are therefore the tiniest of the tiny within the tiniest of the tiny. At the same time, we tower over very small things as much as very large things tower over us. Thus, the cells in our bodies are invisibly small. At least a thousand human cells would fit into a grain of sand measuring a millimetre in length. We are huge in relation to our cells but the latter are huge in relation of the atoms of which they are composed. Within each human cell there are as many as 200 trillion atoms. Clearly, our hugeness in that direction must be balanced with our tininess in the other direction.

We are therefore at the half-way house in the scheme of things. Our centrality enables us to take equal account of both directions. We are indeed at the centre of the universe in that sense. At this position we can mediate between all other forms of life, both big and small. By putting them all in their place and valuing them all accordingly, we ascribe cosmic significance to all life-forms as well as ourselves. Also, at this intermediary position, increasing order and beauty are created not only by us but also by other intelligent beings, assuming they exist in the universe.   As a result, we are contributing to the cosmic unity reflecting the increasing orderliness that will possibly save the universe from its ultimate fate of total dispersal and heat death. This cosmic unity is the dénouement of prospectivism as is now argued.

5. Striving for Cosmic Unity

The Fifth Principle of Prospectivism

A belief in life means believing in the universe's unifying processes that produce it. A belief in humanity means contributing to these unifying processes to make a better future for ourselves and other life forms.

The Unifying Processes of the Universe

Life is ultimately a striving for the unity which the universe left behind when it exploded into being from the simplest form of unity. This is what science seems to be telling us. Each life-form maintains within itself, for as long as it lives, an orderliness that counters the disorderliness of the universe. The universe began as simple orderliness and has been increasing in disorder ever since. It is moreover a fundamental feature of the universe that things come together to form unities. This is the effect of the four fundamental physical forces – the strong and weak atomic forces, the electro-magnetic force and the gravitational force. These forces have created an ever increasing orderliness in the complexity of entities brought into being by these forces. This complexification process has culminated in the complex life-forms now living on the surface of the Earth. This view is supported by the evidence given us by astronomy, physics, astrophysics, cosmology *et al*.

The universe is full of unities of which life and humanity are among the most developed and complex of them all. We came out of unities – initially a single universe and latterly a single cell – and we are striving in many respects to return to unity. The universe began as one thing and has been steadily multiplying and expanding its contents apparently *ad infinitum*. It is running down into an entropic state of disorder. On the other hand, the advent of living things indicates an opposing trend that gives rise to negative entropy. We have therefore two opposing trends:

From the one to the many. The universe began as one simple, unified orderly thing that erupted into a chaotic, disordered confusion of stars and galaxies whizzing away from each other.

From the many to the one. Life can take upon itself the purpose of creating order among the many and return the universe to the unified state which marked its beginning.

Thus, the basic trend of the universe is from the extreme order that marked its beginnings to the increasing entropic disorder and chaos which we now see developing around us. Responding to that, life and humanity are collectively tending towards unity and wholeness, and we are using the light of the universe to get there – in our case, it is the effects of the sun's rays that make all life possible on Earth.

54

The unity that we and all living beings are aiming for is in direct antithesis to the increasing chaotic disorder that the universe is otherwise falling into. This unity - this one thing - lies well before us in the future. It has often been called 'god' but it is only an abstract goal without content and without effect on us in the present. It is no more divine than the 'metacosmia' of Epicurus, who placed the gods conveniently in 'between worlds' and well away from human affairs. It is only a tendency towards the future to which we are all contributing by organising our lives and by bringing order, reason and meaning into existence. The idea of cosmic unity exists only potentially. Its possibility depends on the continuous development of *the cosmos* which represents all human activity in the present. Cosmic unity differs from the cosmos in being perasic (from the Greek 'perasis' a going beyond) meaning that it belongs beyond in the future. The trend is illustrated as follows:

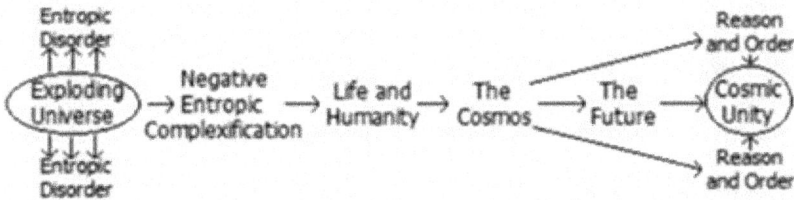

This rough diagram shows the universe exploding into 'entropic disorder' which is happening all around us. Against that trend, a complexifying strand of 'negative entropy' has led to the heavy elements such as carbon that forms the basis of life. Though everything in the universe falls apart eventually, there is an accumulation of complexity that is passed on. Likewise, life contributes to this growth in complexity, as we do as individuals when we add to humanity's accumulated experiences.

When life emerged out of the natural complexifying processes of the universe, more complex life-forms became possible, and humanity is arguably the most complex of all life-forms so far. Humanity's complex social activity has given rise to 'The Cosmos' which incorporates all our reasonable and orderly activity in which we are creating and making things. After that 'The Future' can lead toward greater 'Cosmic Unity' by means of 'Reason and Order' which life, and especially intelligent beings, can bring into the universe. By 'reason' is meant not only logical reasoning but all our inductive and intuitive reasonings. This includes not only the progress of scientific knowledge and understanding but also art, literature, engineering and every activity that can be put into meaningful words, symbols, images and physical objects. This is all ordering of one sort or another. The cosmic unity therefore reflects the possibilities lying before us, assuming we are up to the task.

The cosmic growth in complexity that has resulted in our complex human culture is summed up in the following skimpy progression:

energy → elementary particles → atoms → heavy elements → molecules → amino acids → single cells → multicellular organisms → animals and plants → mammals → human beings → human culture → cosmos → cosmic unity

Energy coalesces into elementary particles, which then come together to form atoms. The constant addition of protons, neurons and electrons to the atomic structure produces progressively heavier and more complex elements. These elements come together to form molecules which culminate in complex amino acids which come together to make DNA possible. The complexity of single cells is compounded by their coming together to form complex organisms that have divided into the two families of active animals and passive plants. The complex social structures of mammals have led to human beings, the most cultured, devious and deadly of all animals. The complexity of human culture surpasses that of all other living beings on the planet, and this contributes to the cosmos when human activities are reasonable, orderly and positively creative. The unifying activity of the cosmos points ultimately to cosmic unity at the end of things.

Starting from energy, each of the entities referred to in the above progression have an internal structure which is progressively more complex than the ones coming before. The physical forces mentioned before (on p.54), have brought the earliest entities into existence as unified structures. But even the most complex entities only preserve their unity for a limited period of time, during which they are centres of order and harmony. At each stage in the complexification process, the entities acquire more powers to establish order and harmony within themselves. These powers result from increasing interactions between the parts comprising them, and the powers are used when they act purposefully in feeding themselves, in reproduction and in combating other entities such as viruses and bacteria that threaten their existence.

Though death and dissolution are ubiquitous and unavoidable, whatever is left behind is not lost as it is available to whatever incorporates the contents of the defunct entity. Nothing lasts forever but while it does last, it accumulates unique attributes that enrich the whole after death or dissolution. This is as true of stars as it is of living beings. But the complexity of living beings means that they have more to contribute to their successors after their dissolution. Thus, death has no sting since it contributes to the accumulative trend towards ultimate togetherness that is possible in the future and will be witnessed by posterity (see pages 33-37 for more on this).

The Unifying Function of Purposefulness

The advent of life has clearly brought purposefulness into being. The single cell organism acts purposefully as an agent in initiating activity for reasons connected with itself and its future survival or replication. Non-life forms cannot act purposefully as they are insufficiently organised internally to generate purposes. Thus, a virus is only a life form in that it can reproduce in propitious circumstances. As its function is entirely confined that purpose, it has virtually no inner life of its own.

The simplest life form brings order into being in fulfilling its purposes. There is orderliness in its internal workings as its metabolic processes are highly organised to ensure its survival. It sorts external things into eatable and non-eatable things and it increases orderliness in its constant replication of itself. In short, reproduction enables life forms to perpetuate the order that each individual creates within itself.

The overall tendency towards ever-increasing complexity throughout the universe can now be interpreted by us as having a purpose, namely, that of rebuilding the complex unity of the universe over time. Our knowledge enables us to see this purposefulness which we can attribute to the workings of the universe. Until we came along no such interpretation could be made. In other words, there is a complexification process of ever-increasing internal complexity which accumulates over time and is seen by us to have the purpose of achieving ever greater unity over time.

In this way, complexification tends towards the ultimate unity of everything. It may seem paradoxical to link complexity to unity in this way, but this unity contains complexity and the complexity involves internal unity. An interactivity of the unity's parts keeps it together just as our complex metabolisms keep our bodily organs working together by their interactivity. A system of dualist interactions is involved which is described by the dualist theory outlined in my book, *The Promise of Dualism* (2015).

Life can do for itself what non-living things cannot do. It can preserve itself as a unified entity by feeding itself and by its internal, metabolic activity over and above any other activity such as atomic and molecular activity. Its inner activity is demonstrably more complex than that of non-organic entities. For as long as a living being lives, it brings additional unity and order into being that does not exist otherwise. That is to say, its internal activity supervenes all the other atomic and molecular activity that is going on, not to mention the quantum activity that underlies all these. Moreover, all this activity is dualistically interconnected as is described in the above mentioned book.

Every life-form works hard within itself throughout its lifetime to maintain and preserve itself for as long as its genetic structure, metabolic and other internal activity will allow it to live. And this is over and above any external threats to its life throughout its lifetime. The struggle to survive consists in the organism sustaining its unity for as long as its structural integrity (e.g. DNA) will allow. In short, the purpose of life and humanity lies in contributing to the ever greater unity of the universe. But this purpose does not exist and cannot exist without our recognising it and making use of this knowledge to further our prospective understanding.

The great goal of moving towards greater unity in the universe is achieved by the rational nature of the ends being pursued by individual life-forms. The 'invisible hand' of each life-form pursuing its own ends is sufficient for life to make the universe more orderly, rational and systematic than it is otherwise. Examples of such unifying purposefulness lie in bees co-operating to make a hive full of honey, or in a tree organising itself to grow by absorbing water through its roots and by photosynthesis in its leaves. They do these things for themselves and without any prompting or support from outside sources. They are therefore unwittingly contributing to the trend towards cosmic unity that makes sense of what life is all about.

Purpose in general is therefore a powerful unifying force which life has introduced to the universe. Social animals have taken this force to new levels as it brings individuals together pursuit of their common aims. Human beings go even further in their social interactions because they can feel *sympathy* towards each other to a greater extent than other animals. Language enables us to understand each other's feelings and thoughts. We bring a conceptual picture of them into our thinking about them. Thus, we can sympathise with other people because we can put into words what they are going through and thus identify with their feelings and thoughts.

Sympathy is the force that brings people together for friendship and social purposes. It is a more rational force than love which has too many emotional and sexual connotations. However, in identifying with the problems of the other person, the force of sympathy may intensify into affection and ultimately into love and devotion. We may then make too much of people for our own and their good. We are perhaps at our most unreasonable when we are in love, whether with a person, thing or idea.

We not only sympathise with people but also with other animals, with states of mind or points of view, or with an organisation, football team, pop star, or whatever. All these sympathies rationalise our feelings as well as broaden them. The more sympathies we have, the more reasons we have to be decent and productive human beings. They can help us to organise and arrange things according to their value and importance to us. When we organise things we bring order and reason into being, and this ensures that things acquire cosmic significance. In short, all these contribute to the cosmos of human endeavour and ultimately towards the coming of cosmic unity.

The Trend Towards Cosmic Unity

Cosmic unity is only a trend or possibility. It is extrapolated or inferred from the given scientific facts about the universe and how entities have developed through time. It makes sense of how the universe has produced increasingly complex entities by its natural processes. These processes began with the strong and weak nuclear forces, and the electromagnetic and gravitational forces. The purposeful activity of life brought further complexity into being. Finally, human culture involves such activities as sympathy, order, reason and creativity that introduce yet more complexity and diversity into the universe. These activities have created a cosmos of increasing order. Thus, complexification produces increasingly organised centres of activity that trend towards cosmic unity in the far future.

Science fiction might lead us to think of the ultimate cosmic unity as a matrix machine to which we are all connected or as a supercomputer that is feeding us with our experiences. In that view, the future unity would be constantly referring back to the present, thus depriving us of our freewill and making our experiences pre-determined. On the contrary, the future is as yet undetermined and seems to be the product of the universe's expansion, as I speculate in my e-book *From Time to Eternity* (Amazon Kindle). If that is the case, the future is yet to come into being and cannot possibly influence us in the present. It also excludes the possibility that time travel might plague us in the here and now.

The term 'cosmic unity' is also found in Buddhist, Yoga and New Age writings. But it is there used in a static sense which incorporates everything in the present. It is equated with absolute truth and lacks the dynamic sense of referring to the future. In that static usage, it has a mystical, religious purpose that is alien to the sense being used here. In this context, cosmic unity is the future end product of cosmic activity via the cosmos, as herein defined (see pages 62 onwards).

This dynamic view of a movement towards cosmic unity makes life and humanity important to the universe in that they both contribute to the unifying trends that counter the increasing disorder and dissolution of the universe. Life and humanity fulfil themselves in unifying themselves. We human beings display our superior intelligence in being better than any other species in coming together to do things. In the idea of unity, we are all for one another. We increasingly interrelate with each other to make ourselves a more unified species. We are one species and only in our unity can we achieve the maximum achievable by an intelligent species and, for example, propagate ourselves across the universe. The idea of cosmos unifies all our activities in the here and now. Our daily activities are constantly creating and recreating it. Thus, our constant contributions to the cosmos are a realistic harbinger of the coming cosmic unity.

In short, humanity's importance is enhanced by the idea of cosmic unity to which it contributes by its creative, holistic and rational activities all of which bring more orderliness and rationality into being than existed before. This contribution is made possible by the cosmos that represents these activities in the present, as is discussed in more detail below in pages 62-70.

The Importance of the Holistic View.

If we are to achieve ever-greater unity, we need to adopt a holistic view which stands outside things and sees them as a single whole. Emphasising the unity of things leads us to look at things as a whole. Everything together makes one thing, and the whole thing makes one. The one contains the whole, and the whole consists of the one.

This holistic view is unique to human beings. We are the only *holistic* species on this planet, as we alone can look at things as a whole, as long as we make up our minds to do so. However, we often neglect this view. Too often, we wallow in the trivialities and irrelevancies of life, and make more of what has no significance in the greater scheme of things. Prospectivism aims to make the holistic view a more intimate part of our everyday thinking. It does so through the idea of cosmos which functions as the day-to-day repository of human activity of all kinds.

Other animals are too rooted in the here-and-now to see the bigger picture. They are governed more by instinct and present exigencies than we are, as we can learn by upbringing to be more than instinctive or impulsive creatures. Thus, the holistic view is not acquired by instinct but must by learnt by education and experience. This holistic frame of mind is fundamental to the prospective viewpoint. It is only by looking at things as a whole that we can achieve a balanced view of our future prospects.

The holistic view is incompatible with extremism of any kind. The extremist typically focuses on one view to the exclusion of all others. Anyone taking the whole view cannot regard one view as being the whole truth of the matter when its merits and demerits are seen in relation to opposing views. The holistic view combats extremism by incorporating dualist view and its appreciation of opposing points of view. Extremism results from one point of view being favoured to exclusion of all opposing ones. It is a monist view whereas dualism takes account of opposing views. However, dualism has the problem of discriminating or judging between these points of view. The holistic view steps outside these points of view and facilitates decisiveness as to which is to be preferred. Thus, anyone who is not holistic-minded can be vulnerable to extremism. A good test of whether a person is vulnerable to an extremist mentality is to ascertain the extent of their broadmindedness and openness to alternative ways of thinking.

Neither science nor religion looks at things as a whole. They cannot give us the whole picture. Science is too specialised and religion is too otherworldly. The holistic view avoids scientific specialisation on the one hand, and religious unworldliness and credulity on the other hand. It is not specialised in that it is all-embracing and all-encompassing. It is not unworldly and credulous as it takes us into the real world to do the best that we can as individuals and to make it a better place to live in and prosper. Holism gives us an informed wisdom that is ever open to continuous development in the light of further thought, experience and information. It gives substance to the practical kind of wisdom characteristic of wise men down the ages. It is therefore a philosophy to be taught and understood; it is not a religion to be preached or believed in uncritically. Philosophy is an active exploration of our thinking in the name of truth but without being the absolute truth in the way that religion tends to be. Similarly, prospectivism explores past truths with the future in mind and is ongoing without being conclusive.

From the holistic viewpoint we can ascertain the extent of our ignorance of things. We can't do anything about our lack of knowledge and understanding unless we see the full extent of our ignorance. What we do not know can never be grasped without stepping outside ourselves and broadening our imaginations in that way. Holism takes account of all points of view without promoting any single viewpoint as being the answer to everything. It is a philosophy which involves thinking about things critically and carefully. The holist can never be a single-minded demagogue or charlatan enforcing his views on other people. He can only be a teacher and never a preacher.

Moreover, the holist view does not reduce the individual to the whole. It does not mean that the state or society is more important than the individual. On the contrary, it is suffused with the Autonomy Principle which states that each individual is an autonomous person capable of unique and irreplaceable development. We are all ends in ourselves and the role of society is to provide the framework in which our ends can be achieved. The holist view looks from bottom to top and works from the individual upwards by ensuring that each person adopts that view for their own ends and not because it is imposed from above *ex cathedra.*

The holist view takes in the whole human race and is therefore incompatible with racism that divides people irrationally. We are all the same in being human beings and are all equally parts of humanity. Thus, human racism is the only admissible form of racism. As human racists we function at our best between the extremes of belief and scepticism and between the extremes of (1) believing human beings to be nothing but animals and (2) believing them to be in the image of God. This is roughly represented as follows:

Belief

⇕

Animals ↔ *THE HUMAN RACIST* ↔ Gods

⇕

Scepticism

Some people have more regard for animals than for human beings and put the welfare of animals before human concerns. They may even think that animals are better than human beings. This is an extreme view that does them no credit, especially if they continue to enjoy human society like the rest of us. Similarly, those who put God before humanity are taking an extreme view since they aspire to divine standards beyond the rest of us who are sinful mortals unwilling or unable to live up to the standards and demands of a god hanging over us. The godly view is dogmatically restrictive and the animalist view is sceptically indefinite.

Both the godly and animalist extremes lessen us as human beings. The one subordinates us to ideas or creeds of some sort. The other belittles us and therefore becomes an excuse for doing nothing at all as all beliefs can be reduced to nothing by verbal reasoning and over reliance on words and arguments. We are more than just animals by the fact that we can differentiate ourselves from them in our behaviour and in our feelings. We are painfully aware of what we are or are not as individuals in ways that animals are not aware of themselves. But at the same time we make ourselves in our own image and we need no imaginary entity to look up to and demean ourselves thereby.

The holistic view rejects the extremes of absolute dogmatic belief on the one hand and of insipid scepticism on the other hand. Thus, it is at the middle of things that the problem arises concerning what it is to be a human being and it is at the centre that we must find our answers, as is implied by the scientific, centralist view, mentioned above (see pages 52-53) See also my books *Advancing Humanity* (2016) and *Hale and Hearty* (2016) for more on the topics of holism and of humanity's centrality in the scheme of things.

The Unifying Cosmos.

The origin of the word. The word 'cosmos' is from the Greek, κόσμος, originally meaning 'order' as opposed to disorder or chaos. It was extended by the Greeks to refer to the perfect ordering of the universe. The verb, κοσμεω (*kosmeo*), meant not only to order things but also to discipline, rule or govern. Thus, 'cosmos' originally referred to the divine ability to govern the universe and its contents. It later became associated with the quest of ancient Greek philosophers for the perfect order of eternity, that which is 'ageless and deathless'. This original meaning is here extended to include our ordering of the universe by means of our knowledge, our achievements, our artistic creativity and everything worthy about us that makes us human in the here and now.

The cosmos encompasses not only everything that we know about the material universe but also everything that the human race has brought into being through its cultural endeavours, both mental and physical. It is not God but is only symbolic of what humanity is and has achieved. Just as the knowledge contained in Wikipedia is imposed on no one, so the cosmos demands nothing of anyone. Like Wikipedia, it is there to be used and contributed to. However, it goes far beyond that incomparable (though flawed) encyclopaedia in containing it and everything else achieved by and attributable to humanity. In this way, the cosmist can appreciate all and everything about humanity however adverse he may be to particular aspects of it.

The unifying universe is complemented by the unifying cosmos. Cosmic unity is the trend or goal of unifying processes whereas the cosmos refers to our specific contributions to that unifying process. What is ultimately important about humanity is what we leave behind us. Herein it is argued that, at the final end of things, the cosmos is the greatest gift that humanity can bequeath to the universe since it contributes to the cosmic unity of the universe.

The notion of cosmos is thus the present culmination of all human efforts and achievements. It embodies a holistic view that brings everything together that is significant about us. So far from being a divine notion the cosmos is an entirely human in all respects since it embraces humanity without going beyond it. Its finality rests in making an end to everything we are as human beings. We are all cosmists in making our own contributions to the cosmos whether we regard them to be trivial or important. We therefore advance humanity, each of us in our own way, by our cosmic contributions, and we are all cosmists in what we offer as unique individuals to the sum-total of human endeavour.

The cosmist is also a holist since taking things as a whole means embracing all that humanity has to offer – past, present and future. The cosmist's role is to bestow value on all our achievements and proclaim their meaning and importance to all and sundry. Wholeness implies completeness and what lasts forever is only a part of the whole. What is being done in the here and now is also included. Thus, the cosmos is the imaginary repository by which holists carry around not so much all knowledge in their heads but the appreciation and applicability of it. That knowledge is readily accessible online, in books, videos and the heads of experts but it is useless unless it is appreciated and applied whenever the occasion arises by those who see when and where it is needed. The cosmist is therefore a visionary who takes account of all that humanity has to offer and makes as much of it as his imagination will allow.

As a mere carry-all, the cosmos is not to be worshipped or adulated since it is merely a notion that serves to put the whole of humanity in the broadest possible perspective. Only we as human beings can do this and not any imaginary beings that are only invented by reflecting on our own capabilities or the lack of them. If we are wise, we will try our best to embrace everything without exception in our thoughts and images. Though we may never attain this completely or perhaps only temporarily, we can't stop trying. To stop trying is to start dying. Life gives us no choice if we want to carry on living.

The ultimate nature of the cosmos. The cosmos offers the remote view of humanity that we need to appreciate its ultimate value and significance, and it is important for the holist to absorb and develop that viewpoint. As herein defined, it is the *ne plus ultra* view of what we are and the place we have in the universe. It gives us a humane way of measuring and judging our achievements objectively without having to resort to a divine perspective that is really unfathomable and beyond our ken.

Nevertheless, the cosmos cannot include absolutely everything. It is a human notion devoted to human concerns. For example, it does not include posterity. Future generations can only be imagined to exist as the legacy of our present efforts. The cosmos points to the future which we are constantly working towards in our daily lives. It is emblematic of everything we have achieved in the past and present as a species. Our future lies not in making intelligent robots that would make humanity extinct. It is in building up a cosmos which can perhaps be launched from Earth and reach the furthest corners of the universe. Doubtless, we will do this as soon as move off this planet and spread ourselves and life across the universe. Robots will be helpful to that end which may be their ultimate function and not that of replacing us. Thus, building up the cosmos is a prelude to our making our lasting mark on the universe.

Moreover, we move forward as a species when we take account of everything that we have achieved and strive to contribute further to our past achievements. The all-embracing view of the cosmos is crucial to our progress whether we attain it completely or not. Everything about humanity and its achievements is gathered together in this broad notion of the cosmos. It contains not just the internet but everything else that we have done in creating buildings, bridges, works of art, and so on, as is listed below. It is therefore the ultimate expression of humanity and everything about it. It is the converse of being divine or religious, as it is only ourselves writ large by using a mere word. The notion helps us to bring ourselves into perspective and to see our cosmic importance instead of belittling ourselves purposelessly as religion tends to do. The act of thinking about humanity and our achievements adds to its importance and strengthens our view of ourselves. This encourages us to do all that is necessary to advance humanity and life in general. In short, we see our contributions to humanity as being more meaningful and purposeful when they are put into this broad cosmic context.

It is the individual behaving ethically and purposefully who contributes most to this cosmic advance. Our self or ego needs constant strengthening and belief in life and humanity also helps to bolster the self as follows:

❖   *Self-Identity* – We establish what we are by believing that we amount to something in life and have some to give other people. We are nothing when we cannot refer to anything outside ourselves.

❖   *Self-Belief* – The confidence to be ourselves is increased by being true to ourselves as human beings. Belief in life, humanity and the future can contribute to such self-belief by elevating ourselves and developing an inner sense of purpose.

❖   *Self-Fulfilment* – We find out what we are here to do by developing the best capabilities within us. This is best done by fulfilling one's potential as a whole and by looking at things as a whole.

❖   *Self-Knowledge* – We realise the limits to our knowledge in the constant quest to understand ourselves better in the widest contexts of life, humanity and the universe.

❖   *Self-Discipline* – Nothing worthwhile and lasting can be achieved without the moral discipline required to do our best. Knowing ourselves means knowing how to control ourselves to achieve what is good for us.

Our Cosmic Position.

In the vastness of space, which is otherwise composed of mindless matter and energy, something different is being constructed on our minuscule planet. It is a tiny seed of unifying harmony and order that we are bringing into being in exercising our intelligence and creativity in a reasonable, responsible and purposeful way. We here call it 'cosmos' which in conceptual terms we can contrast with the material universe. It is the seed that can develop further into the future and towards the cosmic unity that is the ultimate goal of all intelligent activity.

The universe is gradually decaying into fragments and mere energy but at the heart of it we, together with all living beings, are unifying agents who are countering this relentless dissipation of matter and energy. Living beings complexify matter and thereby bring meaning and purpose into the universe that is otherwise meaningless and purposeless. We, the human race, are doing more in creating this unifying entity. The cosmos brings together the additional meaning and purpose that we are contributing with our peculiar intelligence and creativity. This cosmos is like a seed that will sprout forth in the far future though exactly what form it will ultimately take we can scarcely image. The cosmos is not a god in the making, as it is only us making something of ourselves when we act intelligently and creatively.

The cosmos is a part of the universe because we are a part of the universe. But it is distinct from it in being centred on ourselves and other intelligent beings capable of contributing to it. The universe is the external reality with which we interact to make our mark on it. What we do in the universe brings the cosmos into being as something unique to ourselves. Thus, we can differentiate the notion of the cosmos from the universe to draw attention to human achievements in a universe in which we are otherwise infinitesimally small compared with its unimaginable hugeness.

The cosmos is more than just imaginary as its use is supported by the evidence of human activity in all fields including the arts, music, and literature. It brings all that activity together under a single notion, and is supported by concrete products of human activity that cannot be overlooked – buildings, books, artworks and so on. The cosmos embraces everything that has happened to us in the past and is happening to us in the present. Its persistence is confirmed by the eternal existence of the past and of everything that has happened in the past. The everlasting cosmos may be differentiated from the universe as containing everything that exists forever, whereas the universe continues to move on into the future and to disintegrate entropically. The differences between the universe and the cosmos may be summed up as follows:

UNIVERSE	COSMOS
Lacking Meaning and Purpose	Gathering Meaning and Purpose
Decaying Matter	Organising Order
Ultimately Destructive	Creatively Constructive
Impersonal and Quantifiable	Personal and Qualitative
Decaying into the Future	Accumulating all for the Future
Indifferent to us	Expressive of us

The notion of cosmos is needed to bring together everything about us that is more than just matter and energy. It goes beyond the internet and all the intercommunications that make up human society. It includes the sociosphere, noosphere and other notions used to depict our integrated social activities. In this context, it embraces all our physical creations as well as those in literature, science, art, music, commerce, industry and the rest. All our buildings, bridges, artefacts, infrastructure, even our gardens and parks may be included in the all-encompassing bracket of contributions to the cosmos. Though it is not divine in itself, perhaps it has the trappings of a divine being in that it refers to everything 'divine' and 'sacred' about us, namely, when our activities and achievements amount to something more than the sum total of its parts and are valued in more than just material or financial terms.

In this context, the words 'divine' and 'sacred' are not transcendent or superhuman. On the contrary, they are holistic and all-embracing notions in the way they are used here. The divine or sacred object is connected to everything outside it by means of these attributes. A divine person is one who is well-thought of and whose attributes are innumerable and sublime without being godlike. My books are sacred to me in bringing to mind all kinds of thoughts and feelings – "my days among the dead are spent" etc. I can live without my books but I can't get anything done without them. They are not everything to me but they make life more meaningful to me.

The cosmos is not God in any sense of the word, but it is a way of moving slowly and modestly towards what we conceive to be a more divine state of affairs than what exists at the present time. It gives direction to our culture and civilisation. We and all the other intelligent beings who know their place in the universe are together in bringing into existence something that embodies everything intelligent and creative about us.

Everything that we value in life belongs to the cosmos and not to the decaying material universe. Whatever we do on this planet makes no difference to the universe at large. The universe is indifferent to our very existence. But what we do is of great importance to the cosmos since its very existence depends on us and what we do with our lives. It is a notion by which we objectify ourselves and all our doings. It is what we are and what we do *writ large* so that we can interrelate with it as if it were distinct from us. It represents us because we are indeed a productive, intelligent, creative species. We relate to it abstractly and it refers back to us at this abstract level of existence. It is an interactive notion which exists in our minds but which takes us out of ourselves in a positive way. We can view ourselves objectively and assess our achievements through this notion of the cosmos. It is more than an object of imagination or fantasy since we can use it to evaluate ourselves and what we are doing. It gives us a goal to aim for, namely, that of developing and enriching the cosmos so that it boosts the possibility of cosmic unity in the far future. Its existence is qualitative and therefore aspirational. We aspire to it as being representative of the best that we are capable of achieving with our lives.

In making our individual contributions to the cosmos, we acknowledge its wholeness and become holists. To make such a contribution requires an understanding of the cosmic significance of that contribution. When the artist creates a work of art or the scientist devises a new theory, they invariably see the wider significance of their contributions which belong to all humanity. When something new is brought into being, the cosmos is enlarged and invigorated. The more we know about humanity, life and the universe, the more we contribute to its content. The cosmos thrives on the activity of our brains in engaging with its contents. It is also vitalised by the additional order, arrangement, symmetry, regularity, system, pattern, and planning we introduce that did not exist before. The act of acquiring knowledge is a form of ordering and arranging material that is brought into and takes its place in the greater corpus of human knowledge. The 'all' is incorporated into the 'one'; the microcosm becomes the macrocosm, and the macrocosm becomes the microcosm. A constant interaction between these outlooks is the basis of all intellectual activity. Thus, holists can be the ultimate polymaths or intellectuals who bring all available knowledge together to serve humanity to the best of their abilities.

The cosmos is therefore a metaphor for all human knowledge, as well as all artistic and physical achievements. It metaphorically brings everything together and enables us to think more precisely and productively about the human condition and our contribution to the universe. The more everything is brought together, the more order and rationality there is in the universe. It is the simplest way to include all the products of our intelligence and creativity that have been objectified in any way. If they are out there for example in the internet then they are within the sphere of cosmos. In appreciating the cosmos, we cannot exclude any field of knowledge that is understood and appreciated by human beings. In the cosmian sphere, the scientist becomes a holistic intellectual and acquires the imagination and breadth of vision worthy of a holistic visionary. The prospective view is therefore keen on promoting the continuous creativity of humanity.

The Cosmic Contribution of Science.

Without a doubt, our scientific knowledge constitutes our best and most important contribution to the cosmos. It is by far the most useful, the most illuminating, and the most far-reaching of all cosmic contributions. Our increasing medical knowledge is indispensable to the future well-being of the human race, and our increasing scientific understanding of the universe and its contents is needed to ensure our survival as a species. It gives us knowledge of the threats to our planet and of the possible means of dealing with them. The value of scientific knowledge to our culture is immeasurable. It is invaluable but not exorbitantly so. It has immense qualitative value but that value does not overarch the value of every other aspect of our culture.

As science is only one cosmic contributor among many, this fact determines its limitations. Its role in our culture is more clearly circumscribed when we see that it stands alongside the arts and other human activities in its contributions to the cosmos. It adds to the cosmos no more or less than anything else. It may eclipse every other human activity in what it can do for us but it is still equal to everything else in relation to the cosmos. For example, the contributions of art, literature and music are scarcely comparable to those of science in changing our lives materially for the better. But they have a human value that goes beyond all scientific analysis. They are equally indispensible to us in making our lives meaningful and enjoyable. Their value is inestimable in terms of what they give us from aesthetic and emotional points of view. They are needed by us in our daily lives and they are not to be marginalised as their loss would significantly diminish our quality of life.

Science is not necessarily 'omnicompetent'. Scientific methods are extremely important in enabling us to understand the workings of the material world. But these methods are largely abstract and mathematical and do not apply to qualitative value that is largely subjective, intuitive and holistic. That value cannot be pinned down by mathematical or logical methods which depend on discrete distinctions being made and on wholes being reduced to their parts. Science is not 'omnicompetent' (as Peter Atkins put it) in that it is not competent to fulfil the role of other cosmic contributors which do not fall within the context of science. It is not competent to tell us what human feelings are all about. It is not competent to measure these feelings or reduce them to anything scientifically analysable. Any such attempts would violate our integrity as individuals. Everyone has a right to their own feelings without their being imposed on them by 'scientific' means. As it stands, science cannot explain everything about the universe and it cannot predict the future of our species. It gives no clue as to what we are supposed to do with ourselves in the future. Indeed, science cannot account for everything due to its indeterminacy.

It is not possible to extend the scientific method indefinitely, otherwise art, for instance, would be entirely mechanical and mathematical and the machines could take over. There is a sense in which all aspects of human culture may be subjected to scientific methods of one sort or another. Statistical analysis is one example of this. But they are equally subject to other methods which are not considered scientific. From the 1970s onwards, physicists have increasingly widened the scope of physics to include not only philosophy in general but also eastern mysticism. Books such as *The Tao of Physics, Wholeness and the Implicate Order, God and the New Physics*, all mark the physicists' loss of confidence in the ability of physics to supply the ultimate answers. But in reality they do not extend the boundaries of science so much as involve a retreat into philosophy and mysticism in search of answers, (as I argue in my book, *What is Philosophy?* [1998] *e.g.* pp. 11 and 14)

From a scientific point of view, the cosmos functions as an interactive process by which we use ideas to interact with the reality of the universe to make better sense of it. We arrive at ideas intuitively and then we test them in relation to external reality. In interacting with the universe through science, and in doing our meaningful and purposeful deeds that add to the order and beauty of the universe, the cosmos comes into its own as being the interface between the stark materiality of the universe and our ideal, subjective thinking about the universe and its contents. It reflects our intermediary position between its vastness and minisculeness. Thus, on the one hand, the cosmos resides between the macro-universe of astrophysics and the micro-universe of quantum physics. On the other hand, it is placed between our ideal musings and the stark reality of physical existence. Ideality refers to our subjective thoughts and speculations that we constantly relate to reality to arrive at a realistic view of ourselves and the universe. The cosmos grows and develops by such interactions. For example, as our understanding of quantum physics increasingly approximates the realities of the universe, the cosmos grows accordingly. The following diagram brings these four relationships together to symbolise their relationships to the cosmos which is centred between them.

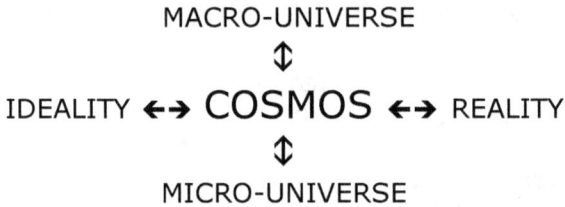

MACRO-UNIVERSE

↕

IDEALITY ↔ COSMOS ↔ REALITY

↕

MICRO-UNIVERSE

An Interactive Cosmic Quadrifoil Matrix

The above quadrifoil matrix shows how cosmic activity progresses interactively. It depicts the four dimensions of interactivity that are necessary and sufficient for the progress of cosmic activity. The cosmos in the middle capitalises on our interactive efforts to reconcile the macro-universe with the micro-universe. We do so by constantly relating ideality to reality and *vice versa*. Scientific research involves constantly relating our ideas to reality and establishing the reality that exists between the very large and very small spheres of existence. We then put scientific activity into a wider context beyond that of explaining the nitty gritty of how the universe works in concrete mathematical terms. Within the context of human activity in general, we can better see its cosmic importance.

The diagram also shows that the cosmos results from the interaction between the physical reality of the universe and the ideal world that we create in thinking about anything, real or unreal. It goes beyond assuming that the universe's reality comprises only the material and physical parts of the cosmos. Materialists make that assumption when they deny the existence of anything beyond the material universe. However, sceptics and idealists may deny even that assumption but in so doing they risk disconnecting their thinking from external reality altogether. The prospective view is therefore an interactive one involving both the real and the ideal. It is neither an idealism nor a realism but involves both of them. Thus, the notion of cosmos reflects the fact that we stay in touch with reality by constantly interacting with it to ensure that our ideas accurately represent reality as far as humanly possible. In short, the above diagram depicts dualist interaction which is elaborated in more detail in my book entitled *The Promise of Dualism* (2015).

The Cosmic Significance of Past Religions.

All the religions of the past have made their respective contributions to the cosmos. The study of these contributions is an intimate part of cosmic research since they all have something to say about the human condition and about what it is to be human. But this is only when we consider them historically. Their cosmic value is lost when they are applied as active vehicles of truth that are set against other religions and sources of religious thought and feeling. Their cosmic significance depends on their no longer being proselytising religions whose truths are forced on people in an exclusive way that brooks no deviation from these truths. We do not need priests, preachers, rabbis, mullahs and the like telling us that holy scriptures are bodies of truth coming from God, angels, aliens or wherever. We want to appreciate the value of scriptural content in its cosmic context not in any supernatural context. Thus, the cosmos is inclusive of all religions even when they are not themselves exclusive. But crucially that inclusion is not uncritical but highly evaluative.

Religious writings make their own cosmic contribution and they include all the sacred works of all the religions of the world, most notably such documents as the Bible, the Talmud, the Koran, Buddhist scriptures, the Upanishads, and the Bhagavad Gita. The range of writings to be included under this heading can be seen in works such as Bouquet's *The Sacred Books of the World*. This book includes writings as diverse as Sumerian Prayers, Homeric Hymns, Zoroastrian Literature, and Japanese Shinto Literature. We can add to this list our growing understanding of ancient religious writings such as those of the ancient Egyptians and Mayans. All these writings are important to our understanding of how human religious thought developed, and of how diverse that thought is. Although humanist thinking has transcended religious thought, the study of the latter helps us to understand the past trains of thought by which we have arrived at a more advanced understanding of our plight and place in the universe.

The cosmos is successor to the comparative religion movement. Within the context of the cosmos, all religions are brought together eclectically with the hope of convergence at some date in the future. This unifying procedure contrasts strongly with the eclecticism and syncretism of past attempts to bring them together. Comparative religion exemplifies an attempt to unify all religions by giving an account of them in a loose and eclectic fashion. No religion is treated as being better than any other though an attempt is made to pinpoint their common features. The comparative religion movement failed because it had no method or system of thought by which all the incompatible religions could be brought together into a unity. The notion of cosmos is a step towards providing such a method of unifying religious thought and practice. It provides a framework within which all religious views and sentiments can be accommodated without necessarily being antithetical to each other.

Religious prophets are those people who have seen beyond the material world and have emphasised the importance of our cosmic musings about our existence. In a sense, we are all cosmic prophets who have our views of the cosmic nature of the universe and who strive to communicate these views to other people. Compared the well-known prophets, most of us make fairly modest spiritual contributions to the cosmic content.

The most important of all the cosmic prophets who have walked the face of the Earth are those who have had the most impact on the history of the human race. They introduced new religions and thereby changed the thinking of humankind by these acts. The most important of all cosmic prophets include Akhenaton, Moses, Zoroaster, Buddha, Confucius, Jesus Christ and Mohammed. Whether the effects of these prophets have been altogether to the good of humankind is entirely another matter. The notion of cosmos now enables us to establish the real and lasting importance of these figures. We do so by accounting for their influence on their contemporaries, disciples, and followers. The facts about them can be studied objectively so that their true value to humanity can be established beyond doubt.

Religious beliefs contribute to the cosmos in so far as they add to our understanding of the human condition. They are to be studied within that context and not adhered to as if they were eternal truths. We can learn from such studies. For instance, the distinctive advances of the Christian message contained in the Sermon of the Mount are permanent contributions to the cosmos. We ought to be *Christians* in our attitude towards our potential enemies and in our attempts to understand people rather than hate them. Equally, we ought to be *Jews* in our respect for family life; *Muslims* in our respect for authority and absolute values; *Buddhists* in our use of meditation to reach our inner being; *Hindus* in our appreciation of spirituality; and so on. In this way, we can make use of the strengths and truths in particular religions without believing in the unbelievable and without practising senseless, superfluous rituals like crouching down abjectly and to no purpose. Such cosmic ideals were anticipated by the comparative religion movement which has its roots in the religious toleration established in Great Britain after the 17th century Civil War. In understanding the merits of religions in general, we can transcend them all within the context of the cosmos. Also, by taking account of all religions and respecting their respective contributions, we pass on to posterity what is worthwhile about them.

The traditional religions clearly have no future as self-sufficient, mutually antagonistic movements. By themselves, they no longer take us anywhere as they have become too ingrown and limited in their outlook and lack competent answers to the human predicament. The exclusivity of these religions means that they exclude unbelievers and heretics. The four great prophets of religion – Moses, Jesus, Buddha and Mohammed – give us great truths but not the whole truth. They got it wrong, each in their different ways. The first and last of these personages made far too much of a non-existent entity with the aim of belittling people unjustifiably and boosting their power over them without limit. Jesus made too much of unworldliness and meekness. The Buddha made too much of introspective meditation to the point of vacuity. Moreover, they all failed to see the bigger picture. Their view of human potential was also limited by the state of human knowledge available to them. Each succeeding generation needs to build on their achievement and not repeat their mistakes *ab nauseum* as the various religions are still doing to their everlasting shame.

To summarise: the cosmos represents humanity's achievements writ large. It is a way of thinking about our accomplishments in the abstract. In being all-inclusive concept, it compares favourably with the exclusivity of religion, which typically excludes unbelievers and heretics. There is no need to believe implicitly in the existence of the cosmos as it is only a means of making sense of humanity's contributions to the universe. It is enough to see its usefulness in that regard and then to dispense with it. There is no point in opposing or rubbishing it as it is only a harmless abstraction that does not require anything of anyone. Its role is entirely descriptive and there is nothing prescriptive about it. If it does nothing for you, it is nothing to you. Yet it is a way of describing everything about humanity and our achievements. It becomes highly meaningful and useful in that context, as it is a holistic aid by which we can see ourselves as an invaluable part of the whole and thus add meaning and purpose to our lives. Ultimately, it is no more than our modest contribution to the cosmic unity to which all living things are aspiring in their own individual ways.

Afterword

This work offers a post religious account of our place in the universe and what we can do in it. For non-religious people, religion is not sufficient to fill the gaps left by science. It only offers comfort through God, meditation, ritual, prayer and the like. In their view, it peddles imaginative nonsense as absolute truth, thus corrupting people's reasoning powers. It is brought into discredit by its proponents who propagate it in an absolutist and uncompromising fashion. The messages of all religions are corrupted when they are enforced on people without taking account of what religion as a whole has to offer us.

Moreover, religion by itself has little to say about the problem of humanity, namely, what is to become of us, given our possible transcendence by genetic, physical or technological means. We need to understand better what it is to be human and what our future will be like, given the possibility of our becoming superhuman or transhuman, of our personalities being integrated into computers, or whatever. This book suggests that we might become less than human by any such developments. We need to proceed with extreme caution if we are to preserve our humanity while embracing such developments.

Humanity can make better progress by inner development than by physical endowments à la *X-Men* and *Superman.* By bringing more life into ourselves we make ourselves more fit for life, whereas by becoming more artificial and mechanical we become less human. We lose touch with our feelings which need to be directed and not replaced by computerisation. If we learn to control our intuitive powers for creative purposes, we will achieve more than if we merely change ourselves physically by genetic or technological means. In short, transhumanism means inhumanism if it fails to deal adequately with the problem of retaining our humanity while trying to change human beings for the better.

This book shows that the materialist view of the universe is not necessarily devoid of spirituality. It has room for a transcendent understanding of the human condition without compromising its essential materiality. This is because life itself goes beyond the merely material in being able to do things or not do them according to internally generated purposes and aims. Humanity takes this internality to its most complex level with our communication and conceptual abilities. This internal aspect of the human condition needs to be fully understood before we can successfully improve ourselves by any artificial means whatsoever. Hopefully, this book lays down some of the groundwork needed for achieving such an understanding.

Finally, prospectivism is nothing if it is not comprehensive. It is an amalgam of 'isms' that include humanism, holism, dualism, interactivism, emergentism, centralism, vitalism, mentalism, to name a few. In all these areas of thought, prospectivism is open to further development and restatement. In pursuit of truth, criticisms are ever welcome. Truth recedes ever before us and demands constant work to keep up with it, especially in the light of further experience and knowledge. Firstly, there is the *internal* problem of balancing all these points of view and dealing with inconsistencies and contradictions. Secondly, there is the *external* problem of constantly relating the material to external reality and refining it accordingly. Consequently, there is no end to it and this is only a beginning.

www.ingramcontent.com/pod-product-compliance
Lightning Source LLC
Chambersburg PA
CBHW060649030426
42337CB00017B/2524